# *The* Complete Survival Shelters *Handbook*

## A Step-by-Step Guide to Building Lifesaving Structures for Every Climate and Wilderness Situation

Anthonio Akkermans

Ulysses Press

Published in the US by:
Ulysses Press
P.O. Box 3440
Berkeley, CA 94703
www.ulyssespress.com

ISBN: 978-1-61243-493-3
Library of Congress Control Number: 2015937555

Printed in the United States by Bang Printing

10 9 8 7 6 5 4 3 2 1

Acquisitions editor: Kelly Reed
Project editor: Alice Riegert
Managing editor: Claire Chun
Editor: Renee Rutledge
Proofreader: Nancy Bell
Index: Sayre Van Young
Cover design: what!design @ whatweb.com
Cover photos: © Anthonio Akkermans except snow shelter © Tyler Olson/shutterstock.com
Interior design and layout: Jake Flaherty and what!design @ whatweb.com

Distributed by Publishers Group West

# Contents

# Introduction

This is a book about shelter, a subject regarded as the highest human priority both in survival situations and modern life. In survival and bushcraft books covering the four basic human necessities (shelter, water, food and fire), shelter will generally be the first topic covered in depth. This is because you can often survive a few days without water, fire or food, but a lack of shelter can kill you within days, hours or even, in some cases, minutes.

The human body on its own is surprisingly badly adapted to survive the rigors of life in all but the balmiest of climes without help to regulate its own temperature. Modern aid and relief agencies recognize this fact by ensuring people in need immediately receive a form of shelter, whether during a natural disaster or refugee crisis.

During my years of involvement with the survival and primitive skills industry, I have often observed people wrongly prioritizing other needs above shelter. There seems to be a particular obsession with lighting a fire first. I have seen people spend hours upon hours failing to get a fire going (lighting a fire without tools or accelerants is a difficult skill, especially during inclement weather), only to find themselves with too little daylight left to construct some form of shelter, resulting in a miserable night without shelter, fire, food or water.

I see the lure of starting a fire. There's nothing quite as comfortable or evocative of times gone by as spending the night in front of a blazing fire with nothing but stars overhead. Though this notion may be romantic, it is also short-sighted. The fire may be hard to get going, draining limited energy reserves. Presuming it gets lit, it will require large amounts of fuel to last through the night (requiring more energy to gather) as well as a constant sense of awareness of when to add more wood to the fire, allowing you no more than a short slumber now and again, interrupted by regular panicked attempts to revive the inevitably dying fire. Spending the night with only a fire to protect you from the elements soon becomes a draining chore, depriving your body and mind of the rest, which is so undervalued yet incredibly important in a survival setting.

# The Benefits of Shelters

Shelter-building may be a less glamorous skill than hunting for food or lighting that fire, but a good shelter will offer you many benefits, some of which may not be apparent at first:

- The shelter will protect you from the elements, whether they be cold, wet or hot. A good shelter will be able to protect you from the lowest temperatures and the heaviest downpours. Just as the shelter will protect you from the weather, it will also serve to protect you from potentially dangerous animals living nearby.
- Your shelter will give you a place you can call "home." A place to return to from your forays. A base to gather yourself together, and a focal point for your day-to-day life. It will allow you to focus on other activities, knowing that you have a refuge to return to.
- Your shelter has the ability to anchor you mentally. How can you be truly "lost" in a survival scenario when you have a shelter to house you and your possessions? A solid shelter is a

tremendous tool to help you retain or regain a sense of control in unexpected scenarios. It can give you a feeling of well-being and increase your morale.

- A shelter will help attract potential rescuers in a survival setting by enlarging your "footprint" in the area when needed. Conversely, a well-designed shelter can lower your visibility where required, giving you a place to store valuable equipment and rest in safety.
- Shelters may be built using only natural materials without any need for tools or modern equipment, whereas many other skills require either tools or handmade resources. (Lighting a fire using the bow drill method, for instance, requires the use of a sturdy string and a knife to carve the pieces.)
- Shelter-building uses mostly gross motor skills. You may be freezing with stiff fingers, but you should still be able to construct a decent shelter. Most other survival skills require fine motor skills and dexterity.
- Shelter-building is a relatively easy skill to learn. By learning and understanding the principles, you can adjust your approach to suit most any environment.

This last point has an enormous bearing on this book. Of course, I will not be able to cover every conceivable type of shelter in a book such as this, let alone cover each in sufficient detail to allow you to build them at home. Instead, I chose shelters that would demonstrate the range of shelters available, and more importantly, the principles behind shelter-building. By showing you the principles at work, you will be able to come up with any type of shelter at all, perfectly suited to the environment you find yourself in as well as your own level of skill, energy and endurance.

Also, I feel that shelter-building in a survival setting (whether self-imposed or not) is in a constant state of evolution. You may start with the most basic of shelters, but over time, you may well be adding on to the basic structure to improve it, or perhaps replace it altogether. You may start with a simple lean-to, perhaps creating walls a day later or building a second one on yet another day. You might even decide to enclose your fire altogether with various structures on all sides.

Learning individual types of shelter is not conducive to promoting a fluid evolutionary improvement of your campsite. Knowledge of the principles at work is needed. With this knowledge, the resources of your shelter site and time available to you will become your only limits.

# Chapter 1

# Shelter Fundamentals

Except in hot weather, as discussed further down, the main purpose of a shelter is preventing excessive heat loss. Heat can be lost through conduction when your body is touching a material that is colder than you. This can happen when you're lying directly on cold ground, are wearing wet clothes or are covered in damp leaves.

Heat can also be lost through convection. Convection occurs because moisture evaporating off your skin requires heat. When you are sweating or wet and the wind blows over your skin, the liquid will evaporate, using heat from your body to do so.

Finally, heat is lost through radiation. Heat always flows from warmer to colder masses, so even on windless, dry days, if the air is cool, your body will lose heat by radiating it into the surrounding air much like a radiator will warm a cold house.

Extrapolating your basic shelter requirements from these three causes of heat loss, your shelter should be dry, insulated from the cold ground, windproof and surrounded by heat or sufficiently low-volume air so your body can easily heat it.

In the exceptional case where you're trying to prevent moisture loss or heat build-up, such as what might happen on a hot summer's day or in a desert, the same principles still apply, only the flow of heat is reversed. You must avoid conduction of heat by not touching hot objects and use convection to keep the body cool (yet in such a way you don't lose too much moisture). This is done by wearing appropriate clothing that allows perspiration, but keeps you cool and dry at the same time. Avoid radiation, again to avoid heat built-up and excessive loss of moisture by staying out of the sun.

Most of you will be concerned with heat loss, most of the time. So in this chapter, I will focus mainly on preventing heat loss and save the topics of moisture retention and overheating when covering specific shelters designed to combat those issues.

# Shelter Starts with Good Clothing

Most people barely give their clothes a second thought beyond fashionability, comfort or suitability in particular social situations. However, the various clothes you decide to wear on any given day combine into your most important form of shelter.

Because clothes are so close-fitting to the body, choosing the right clothes to shelter you from the elements can be tricky at times as you strive to maintain a perfect balance between heat retention and loss. While you want to prevent most of your body heat from radiating into the surrounding air, you must also ensure that enough heat radiates away to prevent you from sweating. Sweating can make you wet, so you lose heat through either conduction (cold clothes) or convection (sweat evaporating off our skin or clothes).

This is best exemplified with people in extremely cold conditions dressing up extremely warmly, using multiple layers of clothes, then removing layers as soon as they undertake any form of strenuous activity. When the activity is over, they put the layers back on. I recall working in nothing more than a single merino wool base layer when sawing and chopping logs for my fire in the Yukon winter at −50°F!

This balance between heat and cold becomes even harder to maintain when factoring in rain.

I'm sure most of you have experienced dressing up in warm, waterproof clothes on a cold rainy day where you ended up wet and freezing because the waterproof coat caused you to sweat so much!

First of all, you have to realize that there are no perfect, all-weather clothes out there. They do not yet exist. Different clothing materials are better at some things than others. The key to maintaining that happy equilibrium between hot and cold then becomes wearing many different layers of clothes, combining the best qualities of different materials. This includes clothes to wick away your sweat, clothes to keep you warm and clothes to keep you dry and protected from wind. You then simply add or subtract layers as your circumstances change.

Below is a list of suggested clothing materials for different purposes:

# Base Layer

Let's start with a base layer. The purpose of this layer is to keep you dry by wicking away sweat. These would ordinarily be worn over underwear.

**Cotton**—Cotton can be very good at wicking away sweat, though it loses its insulative properties when wet and can cause you to feel cold once you slow down. Cotton can also take a long time to dry. It is best to avoid cotton if you have to dress warm and plan to engage in any activity at all.

**Linen**—Linen is very good at absorbing moisture so it can reduce the effects of sweating. It is most useful worn as both the inner and outer layer, as it dries extremely fast when exposed.

**Wool**—Wool, especially in thin merino wool clothes, is excellent at wicking away moisture and also tends to retain most of its ability to keep you warm, even when wet. This makes it one of my favorite materials for base layers. Modern manufacturing processes mean that wool clothes don't have to be itchy as they once were and can be comfortably worn on bare skin.

**Artificial fibers**—Fibers such as polyester and polypropylene make excellent base layers and have emerged in many different shapes and forms in recent years. When choosing sizes, you'll want to make sure that this layer is close-fitting and long enough to prevent gaps or exposed skin, even when bending or stretching.

# Mid-Layer

The second group of layers, the mid-layer, is sometimes referred to as the insulation layer as its primary function is to retain body heat. These layers can be made out of a huge variety of materials.

**Down-filled clothes**—These are absolutely excellent at retaining heat. They're also light and can easily be compressed for storage. They can be purchased with different amounts of filling, allowing you to choose a level of insulation as required. Though they are very warm, they lose most of their insulative ability when wet. Down-filled clothes are best used in extremely cold but dry environments.

**Fleece**—Fleece and its variants are excellent as a mid-layer, even when wet. The one major downside for the outdoor enthusiast is that clothes made out of this material are very flammable and can melt into the skin, causing horrific burns. Steer well clear of fire when wearing fleece, or remove the fleece or cover it up with less flammable clothes otherwise.

A large variety of fleece materials are becoming available in unlimited forms. Fleece clothes are available in different thicknesses. Personally, I prefer wearing more of the thin layers than fewer thick layers as it is easier to regulate temperature by adding or removing a thin layer.

**Cotton**—Often mixed with synthetic fibers, cotton is also a very common material for mid-layer clothes and is extremely versatile. Cotton clothes are useful as they can range from thinner (cooler) to thicker (warmer) clothes, allowing you to layer different types. Again, as with the base layer, the main drawback of cotton is that it becomes quite heavy and loses its ability to insulate if it becomes wet, though the mixing in of synthetic fibers helps to some extent. While you will presumably be wearing a coat over cotton tops in inclement weather, trousers are usually left exposed unless the weather is really bad. For that reason, cotton trousers (such as jeans) are best completely avoided. Instead, use trousers made from synthetic fibers, which are designed to remain light and dry quickly. You will also be able to buy such trousers with fleece lining or removable trouser legs.

**Wool**—Wool can be very useful as a mid-layer, though you may be too hot wearing a woolen top and too cold taking it off. Heavy wool is best used in colder environments or when inactive for extended periods of time. Most wool clothing was replaced by fleece when it became available.

# Outer Layer

The outer layer of clothes, often referred to as the "shell layer," should be water and windproof, be resistant to wear and tear, and allow the escape of moisture (sweat). Most of these properties can be combined in modern jackets made out of materials coated with a membrane. Gore-Tex, Pertex, eVent and other brands offer this option. These membranes can be coated onto many different types of fabric, so you should be able to find a fabric that suits you most depending on your required comfort level and tear/abrasion resistance.

It is best to avoid rubbers or plastics. Though they are perfectly water- and windproof, they do not allow sweat to evaporate and will make you wet (and ultimately cold) from sweat. Breathable fabrics such as the ones made by the brand names mentioned above still need regular treatment with water-repelling sprays. These sprays are not meant to stop water from penetrating the cloth (as the membrane is waterproof), but to ensure liquid forms "beads" and runs off, leaving the pores of the membrane clear to allow the evaporation of sweat.

As an aside, many companies now produce outdoor coats and jackets with a removable fleece liner, which allows you further flexibility to increase or decrease heat retention. When gauging size, you'll want to be sure that your shell layer covers you entirely with no gaps in protection, even when stretching or bending over.

Personally, for a trip into the outdoors, I like to wear a long-sleeve merino wool base layer with a comfy cotton T-shirt over the top. As an outer layer, I use a fleece-lined waterproof jacket. Then, for colder days, I add a fleece or cotton sweater, while for warmer days, I lose the fleece lining of the jacket and perhaps the merino wool base layer. Of course, none of these layers is set in stone, I simply pick and mix as conditions require.

The trick is to not wear one super-thick layer trying to do every job, but a large array of thin layers, each with its own advantages, which can then be added onto or subtracted from to gain the protection you need.

Of course, it may very well happen that you are caught out with too few clothes on. One simple trick to adding insulative properties to your clothes in an emergency is simply to pull your socks over the trouser legs, tuck your T-shirt into your belt and fill your trouser legs and shirt with crumpled-up newspaper, car seat foam, (dry, non-toxic) leaves, or whatever else you can get your hands on. Just be sure to avoid stinging nettles or holly!

# Other Clothing Items

Other clothing items to consider are socks, shoes or boots, gloves and hats.

**Socks**—Just like other clothes, socks come in a large variety of materials. Most outdoor socks are made using a blend of materials, such as merino wool combined with nylon or other artificial fibers. Many companies also produce their socks without any seams or with seams that are relocated to improve comfort and reduce blisters. It is worth testing several different types of socks to find ones you're comfortable with, especially since they come in different weights. It is now even possible to purchase waterproof yet breathable socks, though I have never tried them, so I don't know how comfortable or successful they are. Watch out for socks being too tight around the leg, as this can reduce blood flow. Multiple pairs of socks can be worn, assuming your footwear is spacious enough. One thing to keep in mind is that your feet will generally always get damp when engaging in any length of a hike. Boots will never be able to allow all of the perspiration being generated by the foot through, so pick your socks with this in mind.

**Shoes and boots**—As far as insulation goes, look for an integrated package of the mid-layer and outer layer of the clothes we discussed earlier: warming, moisture-wicking inside and waterproof and durable outside. Manufacturers produce a wide variety of outdoor footwear. Many people will pick lighter shoes for walking and heavier boots for hiking and camping. If you can only pick one pair, I would stick with a good three-season boot.

Within these ranges of footwear, you generally have a choice between fabric or leather boots. Fabric boots are usually lighter as they are made out of a combination of suede and synthetic fibers combined with some form of breathable lining, such as Gore-Tex laminated fabric. I find shoes and boots made out of this material are generally warmer, though they tend to offer less protection upon impact with branches, rocks, etc. They also tend to be a bit more difficult to maintain well.

Leather boots are somewhat heavier and can be a little bit colder, but are generally longer lasting, especially if well maintained with leather wax or similar treatment.

Being particular about the boots you buy is well worth it, as you will have to make do with the pair you choose to wear, whereas clothing can be changed to suit.

Apart from choosing the type of boot, achieving the best fit is also important if not more so. I strongly recommend bringing a sample pair of your usual outdoor socks with you for fitting shoes. While wearing the socks and standing, place your foot in the boot and, leaving the laces untied, slide your foot forward so you touch the front of the boot with your toes. If you can slide a finger into the boot behind your heel without any force, that's the first indication that you've found the ideal size. . The next test is to stand as you normally would in the shoe or boot, tie up the laces and walk around. You may find your heel lifting slightly from the sole of the boot, but provided that it is no more than about a finger's width, this is normal and will often stop happening once the shoes or boots get worn in. Other than that, the boot should feel comfortable, your foot should feel well supported and your toes should have freedom to move about a bit.

It is very important not to buy shoes that are too small, though you can usually get away with buying a pair that's slightly larger than ideal.

For extremely cold conditions, it is important to pick footwear with flexible soles and a maximum amount of room inside for the toes so the foot can move about. Picking footwear which allows the foot to flex naturally while walking is very helpful when trying to avoid cold toes. It may even be worth it to make your own. At home I have a pair of self-made moose leather and canvas boots/ moccasins lined with felt, which are far more successful keeping my feet warm at −50°F than any other boot or shoe I have ever tried (so long as they're kept dry).

Gloves—Here I look for similar properties as the shoes. A soft, warm and comfortable inside and a waterproof, durable outside. There are several manufacturers out there such as Sealskinz or Dexshell, who produce waterproof yet breathable gloves. On occasion, I use such gloves and wear mittens over the top when not using my hands much in extreme cold. When I require the dexterity of my fingers, I simply temporarily remove the mittens. Again, making sure that your gloves are roomy enough for you to be able to move your fingers around is important as it helps stop your fingers from getting cold and stiff. It's also possible to get warm mittens where all fingers except the index finger and thumb are together, combining warm mitten-like conditions with dexterity.

Hats—You can't beat a simple fleece or wool hat combined with the use of a waterproof coat/hood when required. In extreme cold, faux fur or fur-lined hoods and hats are excellent choices. You should also consider having a good scarf available for outings. My personal favorite is a tubular scarf that pulls over the head and contains extra cloth at the bottom of the "tube" to cover my back and chest, just at the places where drafts can sometimes get in via the coat zipper.

# Sleeping Equipment

This section is about the sort of equipment you need inside the tent, hammock or shelter to complete your insulation from your surroundings. Even when you have a tent that allows for a wood-burning stove, you should not forget that there's really only a thin layer of canvas separating you from the weather. Tents in general do not hold much heat. Quite often, the warmth that you sense inside a tent is merely the absence of wind. As such, it is really important to choose the right equipment for inside the tent, mainly to prevent you from losing heat through the ground or the surrounding air. Although primitive shelters can provide great insulation, in some cases even to the extent where modern insulation is not needed, many shelters will benefit from some form of sleeping equipment.

# Tarps and Bashas

Where the ground is wet, any tarp or basha will help you to stay dry. Carrying one in your backpack may cost a bit in weight or bulk, but in addition to giving you a dry place to sit, the tarp can also be used during the day to gather materials, create a dry space to stand up outside the tent or shelter, or even be worn like a poncho to keep the worst of the rain off you when traveling. With this in mind, I feel that often, it is well worth it to carry a small tarp or basha along. An even lighter, though less rugged, alternative may be an emergency reflective blanket. Bashas and emergency blankets are covered more in-depth in future chapters.

# Sleeping Mats

It is also important to carry a good sleeping mat. Unless you are using a hammock or natural bedding as you would in some of the primitive shelters, bring a sleeping mat to both soften your sleeping area and stop body heat from seeping away into the ground. Do not rely on a sleeping bag alone, as the loft will be compressed below your body, seriously impairing its insulative properties.

There are three general types of sleeping mats, each with its benefits and drawbacks.

**Open-cell foam mats or pads**—These are softer and more comfortable to lie on. The main drawback is that these pads are capable of absorbing water, and because they are softer, they have to be bulkier to compensate. Many pads used by the armed forces are open-cell foam mats. If you choose to use one of these pads, make sure it's close to an inch or more in thickness. NATO mats are a good option. Where the ground is wet, make sure to use a tarp or basha underneath.

**Closed-cell foam mats**—Closed-cell foam mats do not absorb water and retain heat better. However, they tend to be very hard and do not cushion very well on uneven ground. They may work better on softer ground or in hammocks.

**Self-inflating pads**—These often contain a layer of open-cell foam inside and an airtight outer shell. When the valve is open they tend to self-inflate to some extent, and this can be topped up by blowing the pad up further. These pads are probably the most comfortable and useful pads out there, though they tend to be a bit more expensive. They pack up quite small, though may be slightly heavier than other types of mattresses. Their main drawback is that they can easily puncture or start leaking air with age.

Though the self-inflatable pads are more comfortable, pack up smaller and don't absorb moisture, the potential for leaks usually makes me go for the dependability of open-cell foam pads.

# Sleeping Bags

A sleeping bag is usually the first piece of equipment that people think of when planning a camping trip. Even though the options in the shops can be overwhelming, choosing the right sleeping bag is actually fairly simple.

**Shape**—We all remember the rectangular sleeping bags we used for sleepovers when we were children. Well, these bags are still available. They are very suitable when the weather is mild, when camping in hostels or accommodations with bunk beds, and when packing space is not at a premium. For most wilderness activities, however, they are not very suitable.

The most commonly used shape for sleeping bags intended for the outdoors is the mummy shape. The mummy bag closely follows the contours of the body. You may remember reading in the earlier chapters how natural shelters should be as small as possible so the body has little space to heat. Well, this is the principle used in this sleeping bag design, to great effect. This is a very warm design, and because the bag is as small as possible, it will take up the smallest amount of space in a backpack. These sleeping bags are ideal for most trips into the wilderness.

**Material**—A lot of very expensive bags are filled with down, particularly white goose down. A far-superior insulating material, down requires a lot less weight to provide the same amount of insulation as a non-down bag. This makes down sleeping bags a lot lighter. They also compress a lot more, leaving more room in your pack for other gear. Down also wicks sweat away quite well. The only problem with down is that it will not insulate when wet. Once the bag is wet, it becomes quite heavy and is also incredibly hard to dry out again. Down sleeping bags cannot normally be put in the washing machine, so a thin sleeping bag liner would be a good option, as it can be washed. If you can guarantee that your sleeping bag will remain dry, no matter what, then down is the best option for you.

A lot of synthetic sleeping bags are now available and the technology is improving all the time. At this moment in time, synthetic sleeping bags are still considerably bulkier and heavier than down sleeping bags, though they insulate fairly well, even when wet. They can also easily be cleaned should they get dirty. For most of my own camping trips, I tend to use a synthetic sleeping bag, as it requires less care.

**Temperature rating**—Finally, you will need to consider the temperature ranges the bag will most likely be used in. Around the world, there are a few systems in use, from the "season 1 to 5" system to the "comfort temperature/limit temperature" system to the "Tog" system. The problem with any system is that it can be taken quite loosely by manufacturers. Standardized systems also do not take into account what sort of sleeping mat you will use, whether you are a hot or cold sleeper or what your personal level of "comfort" or "limit" is. Since many people are more familiar with the Tog system due to its use in duvets and blankets, it is probably the more useful guide. The best advice is to go to reputable resellers who have personal experience with the products they sell or to take an experienced outdoor person with you when you go shopping for a bag.

# Choosing a Place to Shelter

Even with the best clothes and sleeping gear, when it becomes clear that you need to spend the night or if bad weather is on the horizon, you will need to build an actual shelter. The first thing that should cross your mind is the location of this shelter. From personal experience, I can guarantee that spending a generous amount of time finding the perfect location will always far outweigh the benefits of building immediately in a bad location. Even if my need is pressing, I will always look for the best place for the longest possible time. How much time you have to look for a site depends on your circumstances, level of experience and self-knowledge (I know I need at least "x" amount of time for building the shelter I need, etc.).

The main exception to this is if you are in a situation where you need to be found and rescued: an example is being stranded in your vehicle during inclement weather. In this case, it is most important to remain with the vehicle and turn it into a well-insulated shelter instead of wandering off trying to find a better shelter site or trying to return to civilization.

When trying to find a shelter site, it is important to try and prioritize your needs and wishes.

Depending on your unique circumstances, your priorities may be different, but below are mine in order of importance:

**Safety**—Is the site safe from falling branches, marauding animals (including insects), flash floods, land-, rock- and snowslides, and collapse? If you can't remove the hazard, move on. Other safety issues to look out for: Are you close enough and/or far enough away from other people? Is it legal to camp on this site? Is there enough space for your activities, such as lighting a fire or working on projects?

**Shelter materials**—Are all the materials you need available in generous amounts, or could you expect to find sites with more resources nearby?

This is probably the requirement most often overlooked by my course participants when they choose to build shelters in hastily found sites that appear picturesque but consequently spend hours dragging materials from another area, often leading to a miserable night ahead.

**Drainage**—Is the ground on your preferred site nice and dry, or is it muddy? Is it far enough away from streams to avoid most of the dew and insects? Will it collect rain?

**Weather**—What is the prevailing wind direction? Where would the more violent storms come in from? Are there any natural features in the terrain that could block incoming weather systems?

# FIRE SAFETY

The chances are high you'll be lighting a fire at some point, regardless of your shelter type, so it's worth thinking about fire safety when selecting or preparing a site for building your shelter. Fires should be built on a base made out of rocks with the gaps filled with sand. Be sure not to pick waterlogged stones, as they may explode. The point of building a base is to prevent roots or other materials just below the surface from catching fire. A smoldering spruce root, for instance, can burn for many days undetected, spread the fire to other roots and even flare up above ground many yards away from the original campfire, igniting a wildfire days after the original campfire was extinguished. Building such a base also makes it more convenient to erase any trace of your existence once you leave the site.

It is also important to keep the ground around the fire clear of loose-leaf debris and other flammable materials. Keep your shelters well away from the fire, unless you are building a small fire in your shelter (see page 60). Also, keep the fire well away from trees, shrubs and overhanging branches and avoid using evergreen branches such as spruce and pine for burning, as these varieties tend to throw hot sparks. It's also worth ensuring you always have a means of extinguishing the fire on hand. Water, sand or mud are all good materials for helping to kill the fire.

Sharp rises in the landscape, a forest or valleys may offer protection. On the flip side, while offering protection from bad weather, will your shelter site provide a good amount of daylight? There's nothing as demoralizing as living in a deep spruce forest where you barely see the sky and where the day starts hours later and finishes hours earlier. Your site must be open to plenty of daylight.

**Resources**—Are there many resources available nearby for use once the shelter is finished? Think water, food, fuel, etc. This priority is in fact closely interlinked with the shelter materials one discussed above. Most usually, the sites with the best available resources will be found at transition areas where one type of terrain gives way to another. For instance, where a deep wood gives way to a meadow.

**Impact**—Will your presence disrupt the area too much? Might you pollute streams or ponds with a latrine, causing a hazard with your fire or damaging a fragile ecosystem with your gathering? Might you cause a nuisance to other users of the area? Is your site hidden or visible enough for the circumstances?

**Pleasantness**—Is the site you chose nice to be in? Will it help you feel upbeat and in good spirits? Is the site physically comfortable, with flat and level ground? Does the area contain many "nuisance" (rather than dangerous) insects such as midges, ticks or ants?

While admittedly heading toward the "wanted rather than needed" side of the spectrum, using a site that feels "welcoming" and comfortable will most certainly help a positive state of mind.

The skill of finding a suitable location quickly improves with experience and knowledge of the natural world and the particular environments you regularly find yourself in. In fact, with just a bit of natural awareness and common sense, you can even look at any topographical map of an area and predict to a fair degree the most likely areas to contain good shelter sites. To help improve your site-finding skills, try to consciously identify potential shelter sites when out and about, even when in parks and urban environments, keeping everything from safety and resources to impact and pleasantness in mind. It'll soon become a nearly subconscious process. You will know you're on the right track when the need for a shelter arises and the sentence: "I remember seeing…" pops in your head immediately.

# Materials

This book covers a large number of purely natural shelters; however, some shelters use store-bought materials and some are manufactured shelters. The store-bought materials needed will be covered in-depth in Chapter 3, DIY and Modern Material Shelters, while the modern shelters don't require any additional materials. This leaves us to discuss the materials you may need for a natural shelter.

**Rocks**—Some shelters make extensive use of stones and rocks of all shapes and sizes. There's not a lot to say about them, except to keep in mind the circumstances under which you are using them. You don't want to use waterlogged rocks in close proximity to fire, for instance, as the heat may cause the stone to explode. You also don't want to use weak stone (such as thin sandstone slabs) to form a roof or bear weight. Finally, be careful not to move rocks that are really too heavy to lift, as a strained back out in the wilderness will increase the difficulties inherent to being far from modern civilization.

**Sticks and logs**—Again, ensure that they are not too heavy for you and that they are more than strong enough to sustain the weight you intend to place on them.

In some shelters, certain live branches may be used (such as willow), many of which will sprout roots and continue to grow. Ensure that this practice is allowed and ecologically sound. More on this suggestion in Chapter 2, Making Debris Shelters with Your Bare Hands.

**Leaves and other debris**—The most important rule is to ensure you do not use any poisonous or toxic leaves for your shelter. You do not want to be lying with your face pillowed by poison oak, for instance. You also want to ensure that leaves do not contain spikes or other unpleasant features. A failure to be careful when selecting debris can result in some rather uncomfortable nights!

# THE SAFE WAY TO BREAK BRANCHES

Be careful breaking branches to the correct length over your knees or by jumping on them. Damage to the knee or ankle is common when the strength of a stick is underestimated. Try to select sticks of the correct length, or break them between terrain features, such as two closely spaced trees or rocks. (Beware of flying sticks when using trees or rocks to break sticks, especially when battering them.)

Generally, for all aspects of shelter-building, dead and dry broadleaf leaves such as beech, oak, sycamore, birch and so on are most ideally suited. Some leaves are particularly useful to create shelter from. Beech leaves, for instance, are inherently insect-repellent, and so would make an excellent choice! It's quite possible to work with evergreen leaves such as spruce and pine needles; however, they take a lot of gathering and can be a tad uncomfortable

When you're gathering debris, leave the bottom layer of half-decaying leaves on the ground, as this layer is vital for protecting soil and growth and doesn't add much insulation relative to its volume.

The exception to this rule is when lives are at stake. In that case, I would scrape away all I needed and even resort to pulling live branches off the trees if they contained a lot of leaves.

Sometimes, using live or "green" material is a must, such as when weaving between poles or creating narrow openings or doorways. In those cases, I always take care to use materials that are in overabundance, such as ash shoots, blackberry stalks, etc. Even so, I take care to source such materials over large areas so as to spread the impact of my gathering.

Cord—Cord is not needed for most of the shelters discussed in this book; however, being able to produce cord can be very useful in the creation of shelter and some of the shelters discussed will definitely benefit from the use of cord to reinforce joints. Having access to cord will also exponentially increase the range of shelters you can design yourself using the principles here.

The easiest cord can be produced by simply teasing up the long roots of the spruce tree, which can be found close to the surface. These roots are often many yards in length, and for a quick tie-job, do not require any further preparation. You can refine these roots further by coiling them up and roasting them briefly in the fire before running them through a stick split half way to scrape off the (hot) bark.

This cord (which incidentally makes for a great weaving material too) has enormous tensile strength. Its main weakness lies in that it doesn't like to be knotted. You can (partially) overcome this by tying a loose knot, and while holding the root at one side of the knot, gently pushing the knot itself away from you, tightening it in the process.

In an emergency, you can easily create cord by stripping long green saplings of their bark, refining further by removing the outer bark from the inner, stringy bark. Particularly suitable tree species include willow, elm

and oak. Alternatively, blackberry, stinging nettle, dogbane and many other plant species produce excellent fibers too. These inner-bark fibers can be used just as they are, or twisted into fine, durable cord using the reverse twist method described below. In situations where I was truly stuck for time, I have occasionally pulled down ivy and other vines which, while not the strongest of materials, have helped me out in many a tight spot.

# Obtaining Fibers from Blackberry, Nettle or Similar Plants

1. Gather stalks. You'll want to gather one or more straight stalks as long as you can find them with a diameter of no more than ¼-inch.

2. Split the stalks. Using a knife, carefully split the stalks in half, exposing the pithy center. Ensure you are moving the knife away from your body when splitting the stalk.

3. Peel off the bark. If you are lucky, you will be able to peel off the bark along the entire length of the stalk in one movement. But if the bark is strongly attached to the stalk, snap the pithy center together with its woody sheath outward every inch or so to peel it off the outer bark.

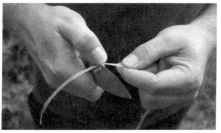

4. Separate the inner bark. As you would scrape a ribbon with scissors to curl it when wrapping a present, scrape the outer bark off so you're left with the strong, stringy, nearly see-through green/brown fibers of the inner bark.

## Reverse Twist Method

You can use these same fibers for producing high-quality cord through a method called the "reverse twist." By twisting fibers together, you will increase their combined tensile strength when compared to the same bundle of fibers, untwisted.

1. Select enough fiber. Grab a bunch of fibers, forming about half the thickness you'd like your cord to be. Pick a spot not quite halfway in this strand, and hold the strand between both thumbs and index fingers, with about an inch separating your left and right hold on the fibers.

2. Initiate the twist. Start twisting the strand of fibers by rolling your thumb away from you over your index finger. Do not keep too much tension on the strand between your left and right hand and keep twisting until the fibers roll over themselves to form a small loop.

3. Twist one strand. Once you have this loop, you will need to change your hand position, so you are holding the loop between the left thumb and index finger with one of the strands above the other. With your right hand, grab the top bundle of fibers and pull them taut, make the same twisting motion by moving your thumb away from you over your index finger. Stop twisting when the fibers are about ready to start rolling over themselves again to form another loop.

4. Switch the twist to the second strand. Now, while holding the twisted fibers taut, grab the free-hanging strand with your right pinky and ring-finger. You should now be forming a triangle with the apex in your left hand. While keeping both strands taught, roll your wrist toward you so that the twisted strand ends up at the bottom, and the untwisted strand at the top.

Repeat this process until you have the length you need. You will know when you don't quite get it right if the cord tends to unravel itself when not under tension.

Making the cord longer than the strands of fibers is easily accomplished by splicing in new strands of fibers about 2 inches before the old strand runs out. If you want to make really even and perfect cord, you can remove a few fibers from the old strand and the new, where they overlap, so the overall thickness remains the same. To create the strongest cord, rather than splicing in new bundles occasionally, you'd stagger the adding in of fibers continuously, a skill that gets better with practice and experience. Ideally, both the individual strands and the cord itself would have a constant thickness along their entire length.

The cord you produced will have exceptional tensile strength. Just be wary of tying moving parts, as the cord does not like the friction caused by rubbing and will quickly fray.

# HAND TOOLS

Some tools that would be extremely useful in shelter-building are, unfortunately, a bit beyond the scope of this book (think ground stone or flaked stone axes). If you have a lot of chopping or cutting to do, it may be worth your while to experiment with bashing rocks together while out in the wilderness. If you want to be well-prepared, enroll in a knapping course and practice. It's surprisingly quick to make efficient cutting tools from stone if you have the skill.

If you are lucky to come across the skull of a deer, you may be surprised by the efficiency of one-half of the lower jaw as a saw! Sometimes shells or fractured rocks can be used for a similar purpose.

# MAKING A HAMMER

A tool worth covering here is a stone mallet or hammer. This can quite easily be made by lashing a stone to a handle.

1. **Make your handle.** Obtain a sturdy green branch about 2½ feet long, and find a way to split it evenly to about halfway up the stick. Use some cord or other strong wrapping material, and create a strong tie at the end of the split (halfway up the branch).

2. **Insert the stone into the split.** Wedge it as close to the center of the stick as possible, where the wrapping you previously did ought to prevent the stick from splitting further.

3. **Wrap the two.** Wrap one of the halves around the stone, and then the other. Use cord to tie it all off. You may have to redo the wrapping occasionally as the stick dries.

An alternative method is to wrap the stone with a larger number of highly flexible branches, wrapping the ends together as the handle. Though it holds the stone a bit better, I always found it annoying that the handle of the hammer often remains somewhat flexible.

# Chapter 2

# Making Debris Shelters with Your Bare Hands

This chapter focuses entirely on shelters which can be built with mostly bare hands and materials found in the wilderness. You will be able to use the principles behind these designs to produce good shelters in the absence of modern equipment and materials. Many of the principles here can also help to improve your experience with modern shelters and tents. The main drawback compared to modern shelters is the amount of labor and time required to build these shelters. However, unlike modern shelters, they don't have to be portable so can be much sturdier and more insulating. It is quite possible to build shelters which can be heated by body heat alone, capable of substituting for both a modern sleeping bag and bivvy bag/tent. More on that in the section on debris huts (page 25).

# 🌿 NATURAL SHELTER 🌿

The first and most basic shelter is also the most important one: the natural shelter. Why spend hours building a labor-intensive shelter in an emergency when you can find one ready-made? After all, humankind lived in natural shelters such as caves for far longer than we have inhabited houses. Indeed, in many places in the world, even in prosperous Western countries, people still live in caves. A case in point is the cave homes near the little Dutch town of Valkenburg. One benefit of cave-dwelling is they tend to maintain an even temperature.

1. Keep a lookout. It is uncommon to spend actual time searching out natural shelters, unless you're in an area known for these types of features. Instead, the trick is simply to keep an open mind and your eyes peeled when looking for that perfect shelter site.

2. Check for animals. When you are looking for a naturally occurring shelter, know that animals may have found them equally useful, so be careful to always check the potential shelter carefully for any signs of use by animals. Signs of recent animal usage can include scat, hair, remains of food or scratch marks.

3. Check for stability. Make sure that the shelter isn't on the verge of collapse. It's wise to poke the structural areas, such as walls and ceilings, with a stick, and later, bare hands in an attempt to dislodge or collapse the potential structure while safely standing outside.

   Natural features offering shelter can range from the overhanging root system of a fallen tree (though often damp) and their trunks to overhanging rock formations and caves.

4. Insulate. Natural shelters are often hard to insulate properly, so a fire or sleeping bag and mat may be required. Alternatively, stuffing a hollow full of dry leaves or making other adjustments may be all that's needed.

 **ROCK SHELTER**

To build a rock shelter, enclose a rock overhang with stones, leaving a small opening. This effort is especially useful in desert regions because the rocks can be heated in the harsh sun during the day and stacked with the hot surface facing inward, releasing heat into your man-made cave overnight when the temperature plummets.

1. Find a suitable cave or overhang. You'll want to find a space which will protect you from the sun and any precipitation. Finding one that you only just about fit in will make for a warmer shelter, while a bigger one may be suitable to heat with the aid of a fire.

2. Enclose the shelter. Wider, flatter rocks tend to stack easier. The rocks can be placed any way they fit, though keeping the bigger, wider ones near the bottom will aid stability. Be sure to leave an opening large enough to crawl through.

Give some thought to creating some sort of bedding to lie on. A good bed of branches and leaves should keep you insulated from the ground. The debris hut below describes bedding quite extensively, while alternative options for bedding are covered at the end of the chapter. Of course, if you are equipped with a sleeping mat, all the better.

To be honest, while this shelter in its most basic form will keep you alive, without modern equipment or extensive adjustments, natural shelters like these will not be comfortable. The heated rocks will help keep the shelter warm, but you should keep in mind that the shelter will be warm only when compared to the temperature outside.

It'll never feel as toasty as your living room. On the other hand, if you find a spacious natural shelter and are able to put a lot of effort and resources into improving it, it can be comfortable and more secure than many primitive or modern shelters.

*The* Complete Survival Shelters *Handbook*

# ❧ DEBRIS HUT ❧

The debris hut is probably the most commonly recommended of the few shelters that are capable of keeping you warm, dry and relatively comfortable without the use of any equipment or a fire.

The shelter uses the insulating properties of still air, trapping the air between piles and piles of leaves as well as creating a space small enough to be heated by your body. The shelter works a lot like a sleeping bag combined with the waterproof feature of a bivvy bag or tent. In fact, in some cases where the environment is damp enough, the shelter itself is capable of actively providing heat through the bacterial action of debris breaking down (a debris hut resembles a big compost heap!), an occurrence quite common in my part of the world, as I live in a temperate oceanic climate.

Debris huts can be built free standing, against an existing structure or in many different shapes depending on your needs. Remember, it's the principle that is important! The main rules for building an effective debris hut are that it must be only barely larger than your body, insulate you from the ground and contain enough debris to benefit from the insulative effects of the air trapped between the leaves. For the purpose of showing the principles at work, we'll cover a freestanding debris hut.

# Create the Layout

1. Scope out your location. You will need at least 4 square yards of relatively level space, clear of sticks, logs, shrubs, trees or other obstacles available on your chosen site. The entrance to this shelter will be at the head end and would ideally face southeast to catch the late morning and afternoon sun and face away from incoming weather systems. If you must choose one of the two, face it away from the direction of the prevailing wind.

2. Outline your body. Lie down on your back with your head pointing in the direction of the entrance as discussed above, and draw a line one palm's width away from your body on both sides of you, starting at your shoulder and moving toward your foot, all the while following your body's outline. Once you have completed this, extend both lines at your feet so

they meet in a triangle about 2 feet away from the bottom of your soles. Also, draw a line to connect the two lines at shoulder level, thereby creating a roughly triangular shape.

This outline will form the shape of the inside of the main shelter and also serve as your template for the bedding. Your head is currently placed outside the triangular shape; however, once the main body of the shelter is built, an entrance will be constructed, which will provide plenty of room for your head.

# Create your Bedding

1. Choose your approach. There are two ways to approach creating your bedding or mattress. You can dig a 1-foot-deep pit and build your bedding in there, or build a 1-foot-high "mattress." In choosing, consider the following: There is a phenomenon known as the "vapor barrier." The vapor barrier is a layer of air right above the ground which holds a much higher level of humidity than the rest of the air. Now, in many climates, this shouldn't matter too much, but if you are building this shelter in a humid area, building your mattress up from the ground can place you above the vapor barrier. Raising your mattress may also be worth it in very rocky ground or extremely cold conditions (cold settles in lower areas).

The main downside of using the aboveground mattress is the added complexity of trying to get into your shelter and its tendency to fall apart at times if you wriggle around too much. The main benefits are reduced labor and a generally warmer and drier experience.

2. Dig a pit. If you decide to dig the mattress into the ground, you will need to dig out a 1-foot-deep pit following the shape of the lines you drew on the ground. Use anything at hand—a sharpish, flat stone, a sharp branch or a piece of bone. You can use the excavated soil to raise the lip of the pit, thereby reducing the actual amount of digging you have to do.

3. Set down the bedding branches. Once the pit is dug, or if you are choosing not to dig a pit, carefully line the pit or outlined area lengthwise with branches from foot end to head end. These branches do not have to be perfectly straight, but should all be roughly 2 inches or so in diameter in order to evenly support the crosswise layer to come.

4. Lay branches crosswise on top of the first layer. Carefully place these sticks side by side so that they fit well together and have no bumps or twigs sticking out, as cushioned by a layer of leaves, you'll be lying directly on top of them.

5. Add the debris. Now, add a 1-foot-thick layer of carefully selected dry debris on top of the latticework to complete your mattress. This is a good opportunity to introduce some ferns (for the nice smell) and beech leaves (to repel insects). Ensure you use only the fluffiest and driest of materials (where available) and filter it carefully to avoid twigs, thorns, seed pods and stones.

# Construct the Main Body

1. Collect materials. At this point, it's time to construct the main body of the shelter. First, you need to select a strong ridgepole, which ought to be about one and a half times the length of your body. Aim for a log that's about the thickness of your wrist or upper arm. You also need two very sturdy, forked branches. The branches, up to and including the junction of the Y, should be about the length of your inner leg. Test them well for strength by purposely trying to break them, because these two branches will support the ridgepole and all the subsequent weight placed upon it! Remember the safe way to break branches rule on page 15 about breaking sticks. Never attempt to break branches using your knee or by stepping/jumping on them.

2. Place the ridgepole. Place the thinner end of the ridgepole right where the two lines meet at the foot end. The two forked branches are each placed in the corners where the shoulders were, the Ys interlinking in the middle in order to support the ridgepole.

3. Secure the ridgepole. When this tripod looks balanced and strong, secure the bottom end of the ridgepole with sticks hammered into the ground on either side and at the end, right where the ridgepole touches the ground, to prevent it from moving. You can add strength and stability to the main ridgepole by fitting more Y-shaped branches along its length, though usually this won't be needed. The overall shape you have now created will be as small as you can get it, while also being of the correct pitch to allow water to drain off. The debris you'll be adding shortly will help it to stay put.

4. Create the framework. Creating the framework that will support the debris is a simple process of placing branches vertically over the original outline of the shelter leaning up against the ridgepole. It is important to ensure these sticks do not stick out above the ridgepole, as this will allow gaps in the insulation to form, or even create a convenient path for water to trickle through. If a particular stick is too long, either place it closer to the entrance where it may fit, or jab it into the ground. You need to cover both sides entirely with these branches. How close they are together depends a bit on what type of debris you're dealing with. If they're very small leaves (or even evergreen needles), then the sticks will need to be tightly packed indeed!

## Add Extra Insulation

Once your frame is filled up you have the opportunity to add some extra insulation to your shelter in the form of an attic, decreasing the wasted space your body must heat. This is recommended in close-to or below-freezing conditions and will not generally be required during spring, summer or autumn. If you don't feel the need for extra insulation, skip to the next step: Create the entrance.

1. Collect materials. You need to find four more forked branches, two with a height of 1 foot and two with a height of about 2 feet, as well as two poles that reach from foot end to head end.

2. Build the attic. Prop the two longer, forked branches against the sides of the shelter at the head end and the shorter ones near the foot end and place the longer poles on the forks so they are lying up against the walls of the shelter, forming two ledges. Place

shorter branches from left to right, through the debris hut frame so they rest on the two ledges. Do this all the way from the head end to the foot end.

3. Add debris. Fill the resulting attic with debris. Make sure to fill the whole space, from the foot end right up to the head end.

4. Add more debris. Another option at this point, if the night is to be particularly cold, is to fill the interior of this framework with debris as well. This means you will literally burrow into a pile of debris when you go to bed. This is certainly warm, but (in my view) rather

uncomfortable and claustrophobic. However, should the need be there and survival at stake, I'd happily suffer a night covered in leaves.

## Create the Entrance

Often, people delay this step until after the debris has been piled on (next step), but I have regularly observed people being too tired at that point to make a good job of it and suffer the consequences once the temperature drops. The entryway just doesn't appear that important once there's a comfortable-looking bed inside a framework topped by a 5-foot pile of leaves and you're exhausted. However, if all the heat can simply escape from the poorly constructed or nonexistent doorway, then all the preceding work will have been completely worthless (apart from keeping you dry).

1. Collect tough but flexible branches. You will use these branches for the entrance. Willow, ash, hazel and holly are some examples of suitable wood. These branches should be at least 1 yard in length. You will also need some form of a sturdy peg and a rock to hammer holes into the ground for inserting the flexible branches into.

   The smaller the entrance is, the warmer the hut will be. As a point of reference, for my photos on the right, the entrance is about 1½ feet wide and about a foot high. The entrance consists of three or four hoops stuck into the ground.

2. Construct the hoops. Place the first hoop 12 inches away from the main frame. Insert one branch into a hole you created with the rock and peg and another one parallel to it in a hole on the other side of the main frame. Connect the branches by weaving them together. Add another hoop 12 inches away from the first one in the same manner, but slightly smaller. And one or two more after that. The last hoop should be about 1½ feet wide and 1 foot tall.

The hoops should then be further reinforced by weaving another number of branches through them in both directions. Repeat this two or three times, finishing with the smallest hoop.

3. Connect the hoops with smaller branches. Add long, flexible branches to connect all the hoops together as well as the frame of the debris hut to form a tunnel. Focus mainly on the roof of the tunnel as this is where the debris will fall through. Use as many as you need to create a strong latticework of interwoven twigs and branches. The objective of this latticework is to prevent debris from falling through.

## Add the Insulation

1. Gather and distribute debris. This step is the easiest to describe, and the toughest to carry out. The thickness of the debris depends on the temperature you expect during the night, but the average 50° to 60°F night would require about 3 feet of debris in each direction from the framework. Do not underestimate the amount of leaves this is! Considering your framework already came to a height of 2 feet (if not more), the height of your shelter when finished ought to be a good 5 feet! I often help myself get the thickness right by laying a few large logs 3 feet to either side of the shelter, so it's easier to judge when the required thickness has been achieved. Spread the debris evenly, creating a large "cocoon." Smooth the debris into a smooth dome so you don't have sudden dips or rises.

Here are a few things to keep in mind:

- On a windy day, add branches over the top to help keep the leaves in place.
- Some people suggest layering the shelter with pieces of bark and the like to help divert rain from the shelter, but I have never found this necessary.
- The debris used for covering the shelter may be wet, rotten, prickly or whatever else. I have even used green leaves when I had no other choice!

- One cheat (which will lower the insulative value) is to lay a foot of leaves, then a layer of twigs, then more leaves, etc. This saves a bit of work, but will cost you in lost temperature.

Try to get your normal human fastidiousness out of your system. In order to carry the largest amounts of leaves to your shelter, you will need to hug the leaves like you would a lover. Do not work by squeezing a small pile of leaves between two palms! It's also wise to gauge how large an area of debris you need and then start collecting leaves farther away from the shelter, working toward the shelter and removing the debris right at the shelter only when adding the last touches. This will help you continue to work when energy starts to get low.

2. Create the door. The very last step is to create some sort of a woven bag filled with leaves, or a big pile of debris which can be dragged in behind you to close the door once you're inside. The inevitable oversupply of leaves inside the shelter can be used to plug any holes around the door plug. You really want to put a bit of effort into creating this door plug. It will never be the same thickness as the rest of the walls, so being able to close any gaps will make a big difference.

3. Enter your shelter. The shelter is most easily entered feet first while lying on your belly, but be sure to tuck in your clothes well, as the entrance tends to undress you in the process of your crawling in! You can fit your body through an entrance narrower than your shoulders by having one arm beside your body and one arm above your body, holding your shoulders more diagonal as you crawl in. Getting in and out of  this shelter will take a bit of time and, if hurried, can easily damage the entrance tunnel. You do not want to forget to use the "toilet" before tucking in!

## Some Tips to Consider

Before using the debris hut, some tips you might consider are heating rocks at a fire (if you have one) for adding extra heat, and smoking out your shelter to help get rid of insects. (See page 66.) It's also worth it to use a thin T-shirt or other clothing item, if you can spare it, as a pillow, rather than putting your face directly in the debris.

Sleeping in a debris hut such as this one does require a bit of adjusting. It may feel slightly claustrophobic with the thought of that heavy ridgepole right above your head. I can reassure you, though, that I've never seen one collapse. In fact, even when trying to dismantle these shelters on purpose, removing the entire ridgepole from underneath the structure does not cause the shelter to collapse. This is because the main weight of the debris is deflected off the ridgepole and frame by the pitch of the roof while the upright sticks of the frame lean against each other.

Something else to keep in mind is that the shelter can feel a little cold at first and you may experience drafts or cold spots. Most often, these spots can be fixed the next day, though the shelter will probably never be quite as hot as your bed at home. The absence of the familiar weight of a blanket can make you feel a bit exposed. After a bit of getting used to, though, you will find that the shelter does see you comfortably through the night. I have found myself too hot at times and often wake up later than intended due to my leafy cocoon preventing all but muffled sounds from breaching it and the absence of natural light.

 **LEAN-TO**

The lean-to is probably seen as the outdoorsman's quintessential shelter. I feel that, though the lean-to has some strong points, its value has perhaps been somewhat overrated. The lean-to is essentially a pitched roof to sit under. Due to its pitch, there is a large amount of "lost" space closest to the ground. It works poorly as a fire reflector and has no insulative properties. If you choose to erect a lean-to, you must have access to a good sleeping bag and mat. Even with a fire, the shelter is cold enough to force you to keep the fire going all night and turn over regularly. Its plus sides are that it's incredibly quick to erect, provides a good shelter from rain (or sun) and is easily scalable into a bigger or smaller structure, as fits your needs. For ease of building your first, the below steps describe a lean-to suitable for sleeping under only.

## Select Your Location

1. Find a level site. It is possible to produce a freestanding lean-to by using 4- to 5-feet-long forked branches, but it's handiest to simply use two conveniently spaced trees with side branches starting about 4 feet high and with 7 feet of space between them to accommodate the shelter you intend to build. When building this shelter, you must definitely ensure the roof

is going to provide shelter from the prevalent wind direction, so select a site that gives you that option or is well sheltered from the wind.

2. Gather the materials. You will need to gather a strong 8-foot-long pole. You also need a large number of sticks long enough to reach the ground and the pole at an angle of about 45 degrees, so gather sturdy sticks about 7 feet long. If they come covered in twigs, all the better for holding the leaves up.

## Build the Lean-To

1. Build the structure. Place the pole horizontally between the two trees, preferably resting on sturdy tree branches that are about 4 feet above the ground. If your two trees don't have two conveniently placed branches available, you could tie the pole to the tree at the right height if you happen to have some cord or are able to make some (see page 16 for instructions), and/or find some forked branches to lean against the tree to provide a resting place for the pole.

2. Create the roof. Once the pole is placed, lean the longer branches against the pole, tightly packed together, to form a roof pitched at about 45 degrees. If your pitch is flatter, rain will seep through and you will have a lot of "dead space" close to the ground, while conversely, if your pitch is too steep, there's little shelter and the debris will slide off. Once the framework of your roof is complete, you can improve debris retention by weaving in some blackberry stalks, twigs or any other material that will snag the debris and prevent it from falling through or sliding down.

3. Add leaf debris. Heap debris on top of the frame, all the way to the ground. In most climates, you'll need to put a 1- to 1½-foot layer of debris on the roof to prevent leakages. If the weather is windy, weigh down your leaves by adding a layer of branches over the top.

4. Improve on the design. There are many ways to improve the lean-to using the knowledge gained from the debris hut on page 25 or shelters discussed later in the book. You could extend the lean-to roof to shelter the sides, stuff the dead space between the ground and roof with debris, add woven walls to the sides, as described below using the stacked debris wall technique, or even create some form of a back wall using stones or logs. The main benefit of using this shelter type over any other primitive type is that it's relatively quick to erect and is successful at its main objective: shedding rain. Assuming that the night is warm and without wind, or that you have a good sleeping bag and/or a fire burning, this shelter should be comfortable enough to sleep in too.

##  STACKED DEBRIS WALL

The stacked debris wall shouldn't be seen as a shelter so much as a building component that is incredibly useful and, due to its versatility, can be employed in many different situations. On top of that, it's also relatively quick to build and, by its very nature, highly insulative. In fact, the stacked debris wall is so successful that we've been building versions of it since the earliest of times and are still using the principle to this day in modern building in the form of the insulated cavity wall.

The structure simply consists of two parallel woven walls, filled in with debris.

## Select the Site and Gather Resources

1. Select the site. Find a clear space, keeping in mind all the priorities for picking a safe and suitable site (page 12). You may want to plan the site to accommodate a larger campsite, so be sure to have enough space for a potential fire and any activities you may wish to perform.

2. Collect materials. To erect the wall, you will need a number of long, straight and sturdy poles, about a foot longer then the height of the intended wall, and plenty of flexible material for weaving. Young saplings, blackberry stalks, willow or anything else flexible will do in a pinch.

If you intend to build a long-term structure, you could consider using live willow poles, as they may sprout and continue growing, adding to the strength and durability of your wall.

## Create the Framework

1. Draw the floor plan. Draw two parallel lines on the ground, spaced 1 foot or so apart from each other. These lines may be straight or curved or follow whatever shape you wish as long as they're always separated by 1 foot. The lines should be as long as you wish your wall to be wide.

2. Secure the poles. Using a large rock, hammer the poles into the ground along one of the lines. Each pole should be spaced about a foot apart and hammered deep enough to be sturdy. Usually a depth of about ½ foot to 1 foot is more than deep enough. Once you complete the row of stakes on one line, repeat the procedure on the other line so you end up with two parallel rows of poles hammered into the ground. If your wall has two ends (like the one in the pictures on the right), place another stake at each end, closing off the wall. Of course, the deeper and sturdier your poles are hammered into the ground, the stronger your wall. However, due to the weaving that will take place, if a few of the poles don't quite hammer in so deep, your wall should still be sturdy enough.

3. Weave the walls. Use the flexible material to weave between the poles. Especially when your row of poles is wobbly, you'll want to ensure that the weave exerts equal pressure both ways. Other than that, the weave only has to be tight enough to contain the debris we're going to throw into the empty space later, but of course, if you have plenty of materials, you can weave your wall as tightly as you wish. If you do manage a tight weave, you could even consider plastering the weave with a clay/sand/grass mixture for a smooth, debris-proof finish! Do not forget to weave around the ends, so as to prevent debris from falling out there.

*The Complete Survival Shelters Handbook*

## Finish the Wall

1. Fill the wall with debris. Once your weave is complete, gather as much debris as you can find, and fill the wall up, tightly packing all available space with debris. I find that using smaller armfuls, and using a stick to "stir" the leaves down after placing them in the wall works best to achieve a tightly packed mass of debris without disturbing the weaving too much.

2. Finish the wall off. Gently compress the leaves and top off the wall with sticks.

## Shaping the Wall into a Shelter

You can easily use the stacked debris wall combined with the lean-to principles above to create a basic shelter. Simply build one long back wall and two side walls.

1. Add side walls. Use the "Create the Framework" steps on page 38 to create two shorter walls at either end of, and perpendicular to the long wall, forming a rectangular space enclosed on three sides. Allow these side walls to become higher toward the front and include two forked branches at the very front, which will support a ridgepole.

2. Build the roof frame. Place the sturdy ridgepole into place over the forked branches. Then, lean sturdy branches over the ridgepole, extending from the top of your back wall. As your wall will sag a little over time, ensure that the branches stick out a good foot or so over the

ridgepole. Try to build your structure in such a way that the roof has a pitch close to 30 degrees to allow water to run off easily.

3. Add debris. Once the framework for the roof is complete, place a solid 1 to 1½ feet of debris on top. Ensure that the debris is thickest at the front and gently slopes down toward the back. On windy days, you can add branches to help hold the debris down.

Whenever I was staying in the woods as a youth with access to a sleeping bag and mat, I would stay in such a shelter, as it was handy, comfortable with a fire, and I could wake up with the sun rising in front of me. I have good memories of using this shelter, including one where a bird decided to cohabit with me for a few days, staying over in the roof each night.

# ROUND DEBRIS WALL SHELTER

After having built such a stacked debris wall, especially with the suggested modifications, it is only a small step forward to use the principles to build a larger, all-enclosing and much more permanent residence.

The debris wall shelter, if maintained properly, can last for many years, as some of my course participants can attest to. It is truly a joy to stay in, even if it does cost some elbow grease to build. The instructions below only demonstrate one way to build it. There are many modifications of shape and size that you can make to the design to meet your individual needs.

You will need the same materials as listed on page 37 for the stacked debris wall, though in bigger quantities. You will also need some cord, string or natural alternative, such as a long vine, to complete the measurements.

## Draw Your Floor Plan

First, you will need to decide on the size of your shelter. The shelter described here will feature a fireplace and will have enough room to sleep three to four people. To calculate the internal diameter, add up the number of feet you need in a cross section. The central fireplace needs 4 feet. Then, on either side of the fireplace, you need a further 6 feet to the outside wall, giving you an internal diameter of 16 feet. As the walls will be 1 foot thick, the external diameter will be 18 feet. Obviously, you have complete freedom to decide yourself what size you'd like your shelter to be instead of using the measurements here, and there's also plenty of room for inaccuracies.

1. Create your drawing tool. In the center, where the fireplace will be, hammer a peg into the ground. Tie a 9-foot piece of string to it (half the shelter's outer diameter), with another peg attached at the loose end.

2. Drawing your outer wall. Being careful not to damage the setup, pull the string taut, and draw a circle by dragging the loose peg through the ground, keeping the string taut while marking. Doing this correctly should give you a perfect circle, 18 feet in diameter, which marks where the outer wall will stand.

3. Drawing your inner wall. Now, shorten your string by 1 foot, and draw a second circle on the ground. This second circle will form your inner wall. At this point, decide where your entrance is to be, and mark it on the ground. The entrance should be between 2 and 3 feet wide and can face any direction you like, though most people prefer it to be south to southwest-facing to capture most of the sun.

## Build the Walls

1. Hammer poles into the ground. Once these circles are drawn and you're happy with the location of your doorway, you can proceed with hammering poles into the ground, exactly as you did for the stacked debris wall on page 37. Make them nice and solid and about 1 foot apart from each other. Don't forget to leave the opening for the doorway. The height of the sticks will determine the maximum height of the wall and, subsequently, the lowest point in your roof.

I like to have the walls about 5 feet above the ground, as this will provide plenty of clearance later to build bedding and still rest comfortably with my back against the wall and the roof clearing my head while seated. You also need to allow for some downward compression of the debris by the roof. When finished, you should have two circular rows of stakes terminating at each end of the doorway. Finish off the framework by hammering in two forked branches at each side of the doorway with the forks facing the entrance, closing off the hollow walls and providing a resting point for the future lintel over the door.

2. Weave and fill the walls. At this point, you're ready to start weaving flexible materials through the stakes to hold the debris you will add later in place. Refer to page 38 for more details about the weaving. You might want to give careful consideration to what materials you use for weaving the inside wall and how tight you create the inside weave, as you may be resting against this wall later. If you are short on materials but still want to rest against the wall without debris raining down your back, consider planning ahead to create a tight weave in the places you expect to be sitting against the wall, and a loose weave everywhere else.

Once the weaving has been completed, you can fill in the walls with tightly packed debris, ensuring that no gaps are left.

# Build the Roof

1. Gather materials. For the next step, you will need to gather four extremely sturdy forked logs. Assuming that your wall is about 5 feet high, the length of these poles (above ground) should be about 6 feet. You will also need four strong branches, each about 5 feet in length.

2. Create the roof supports. In the center of your shelter, measure out a 4 x 4-foot square. This is to become the fireplace. On each of these corners, dig a foot-deep hole in order to place the four forked branches securely upright. Connect these four uprights by laying the four strong branches across them so they form a square. Often, by puzzling carefully, you can create the square in such a way that the branches lock themselves into place. Standing back, it will appear that the roof you're going to place over the shelter will hardly have any pitch at all. This is true initially. However, over time, the heavy roof will compress the debris walls somewhat, making the pitch more acceptable.

3. Create the fireplace. At this point, I like to create a formal fireplace by making a ring out of stones. Place the stones 6 inches to 1 foot high within the four poles and fill the ring with sandy soil, leaving a shallow bowl. You'll want to make sure that the fire pit stays well away from the four supports. I would suggest trying to limit the diameter of the pit itself to

1½ feet. It is possible to build an advanced fireplace at this time, providing more air to the fire, if you wish. See page 60 for instructions.

4. Build the roof. Now is the time to place a sturdy stick (the lintel) across the two forked branches at the entrance and to start laying sturdy poles across the roof from the square in the center to the top of the wall or beyond. Ensure that the poles overlap the square by a good 6 inches, but not much more, to allow for the sagging walls later. In the images on the right, in fact, you may notice that some roof poles are going all the way to the ground, which is not a bad idea, as it adds some stability. You want to start laying poles so that they are equally spaced out, like the rays on a child's drawing of the sun. Obviously, there's only so much space at the square, so when the space fills up, lay poles with the bottoms on the wall, and the top over already placed poles. Continue this process until the top of your entire structure is "roofed" with poles. If you do it right, you should still have a 3 x 3 feet square hole in the center, which will be needed for smoke to escape.

5. Cover the roof with debris. When you're finished with the poles, you can start throwing debris over the top. Place a good 1 to 1½ feet of debris on top. Ensure that the debris is thickest at the smoke hole and gently slopes down toward the walls, creating a gentle dome. On windy days, you can add branches to help hold the debris down.

6. Cover the entrance. With the roof and the walls now finished, you'll need to come up with a way to close over the entrance. There's really no convenient "bare hands" way to do it. In the past I've used hides, clothes or even some old sacking I had found.

There is a lot you can do with the empty space inside. In "Bedding" (page 63) we will talk about ways in which to create bedding and other "furniture" for shelters such as these.

Even though creating a shelter such as this is an incredible amount of work, it is immensely comfortable and gratifying to stay in. These structures can last for many years and be enjoyed again and again. If I had to choose a long-term primitive shelter to build in my backyard, this would be the one.

# FIRE SAFETY

As this shelter will have a fire inside, a word of warning is appropriate here. You should ensure you have the means to extinguish any fire immediately. You're creating fire inside a wood and leaf building. Any sparks flying up can easily land in the debris that forms the roof. It is vital to be vigilant at all times! In my own experience living in such shelters, I have extinguished smoldering leaves in the roof, right at the edge of the smoke hole and have seen roof supports getting charred a third of the way through. Apart from vigilance, regular application of damp clay mixed with a small amount of chopped-up grass to at-risk areas of the shelter can be a real help. It is also important to keep a tidy shelter with equipment stored out of the way so in case of emergency, the exit can easily be reached. In such shelters, I also keep the floor scrupulously clean of debris for fear of a spark landing in it. When possible, I like to have a container of water or damp sand available too. Finally, creating your fire using broadleaf wood only and keeping it small will minimize sparks.

# BENT SAPLING SHELTER

Even though the bent sapling shelter is constructed in an entirely different way, it still uses a number of the principles discussed in the round debris wall shelter. This shelter is circular and can be built using surprisingly few resources. For this example, I'll describe the construction of a shelter large enough for two people to shelter in, though with no room for a fire. Once you build one of these, you'll realize that the shape resembles that of a roomy tent. As the saplings are bent over to meet each other, they create a fairly high space with a lot of room to move about in.

## Draw the Outline and Collect the Materials

1. Draw a circle. In order to build this shelter, you'll first need to create a circle with a diameter of about 9 feet. In the center, hammer a peg into the ground. Tie a 4½-foot piece of string to it (half the shelter diameter) with another peg attached at the loose end.

2. Draw the outline. Being careful not to damage the setup, pull the string taut, and draw a circle by dragging the loose peg through the ground. Doing this correctly should give you a perfect circle 9 feet in diameter, which marks where the wall will stand.

3. Collect materials. It's time to collect a number of young flexible saplings. You need sixteen 9-foot-long saplings, eight 6-foot-long saplings, and a number of spare saplings with a length somewhere between 5 and 9 feet.

## Build the Shelter Frame

1. Create the first two hoops. Decide where your entrance is going to be, and create two 1-foot-deep holes about 2 feet apart using a ½-inch-thick, 1-foot-long branch as a punch and a rock or log as a hammer. Remove the punch and insert two of the 9-foot saplings. Move to the opposite side of the circle and repeat the procedure. You should now have four 9-foot-long saplings sticking out of the ground. Go into the circle, and bend one of the doorway saplings toward you. At the same time, bend the opposite rear sapling toward you. Weave the two ends together by wrapping them around each other to ensure that the roof assumes a nice, dome-like shape. Once you're happy with the shape, grab the two other saplings and repeat the procedure. You should now have two "hoops" running parallel from the entrance to the back of the shelter.

2. Create two more hoops. Now create four more holes, two on opposite sides so that your saplings will make two more arches perpendicular to the ones you already have. If you want and if you have string (instructions on how to make your own cord on page 16), you could tie the four junctions where the saplings cross over together for extra sturdiness. You can also use some of the spare, 5- to 9-foot saplings to reinforce the four hoops by weaving them through and around the existing saplings, which will also give you an opportunity to fix the four junctions together.

3. Build the remaining hoops. Move back toward the entrance and, about a 1½ feet to the right of it, insert one of the 6-foot saplings into the ground. Repeat at the back, and bend and

weave them together to form yet another parallel hoop. Try to ensure that the arch of this hoop meets the original hoops in height. Again, you can reinforce the structure by weaving the resulting two junctions with the previous hoop together using saplings or some cord. Repeat this process on the left side of the entrance as well as twice more, going from side to side. You should now have four hoops going from front to back, and four traveling from side to side. The frame for your shelter should start to resemble an upturned cereal bowl.

4. Create a horizontal ring. Use the remaining 9-foot saplings to create horizontal circles around the shelter frame, starting 1 foot above the ground with the first circle, weaving and/or tying it all together and then traveling up another foot to repeat. Take care not to encircle your shelter completely with the first two circles, as you'll need to leave a doorway open. Once the roof starts becoming more horizontal than vertical, decrease the spacing or even spiral your weave to the center of the roof. Later, you will place debris on top, so the smaller the gaps in the frame are now, the easier your next step will be.

5. Prepare the shelter for debris. Gather a large number of easily woven material such as blackberry stems, and randomly weave them through the entire structure. You can also add branches containing large amounts of twigs to the structure. Evergreen branches are a great resource to use here. The objective is to prevent debris from falling through. The better a job you do with this step, the more comfortable your shelter will be. You could also use any leftover saplings to strengthen your doorway.

## Finish the Shelter

1. Cover the shelter in debris. Now that you've completed the framework, you're back to gathering debris. Initially, the debris tends to slide off, landing in a heap at the side of the shelter; however, before long, it'll start to build up properly, allowing you to cover the whole structure with a 1½-foot layer of debris. Alternatively, you could make a low stacked debris wall for the first 2 feet or so to help hold it all together.

2. Close the entrance. Again, it can be tricky to close off the entrance unless you have access to plastics or sacking, but as we're concerned mainly about shelter from wind and rain in this case, it shouldn't matter too much if the entryway is left open. To block off wind, you could build a wall in front of the entrance. Finding a way to close the entrance should make the shelter somewhat warmer. Since there's no fire inside this particular example, the space is large and the insulation is little, you'll mostly be relying on clothes and a sleeping bag for warmth.

I have always felt that these shelters are relatively quick to build compared to some of the previous ones I discussed. From the outside, the shelter might appear heavy and uncomfortable, yet once inside, there is a surprising amount of space and a certain grace to the structure.

## CORACLES

As an aside, the framework you've just completed was historically used not only as a form of shelter, but also as a boat. Essentially, the poles would be reinforced further by a few rows of tight weaving close to the ground. The frame would then be pulled out of the ground, flipped over, covered in a large cowhide (or sometimes several with waterproofed seams), and used as-is. These skin boats are referred to as "curraghs" or "coracles," and were commonly used in Ireland.

# SUBTERRANEAN SHELTER

Another great and relatively uncomplicated form of shelter would be the subterranean shelter. These types of shelters work especially well in hot conditions or temperate climates, provided the soil is easily excavated. Another advantage is that the shelter is relatively low-profile and can easily be disguised. This may be useful if you wish to remain unseen when observing animals or require a minimal footprint for safety. The main downside is that it can be hard to build if you don't have a small shovel and are unable to improvise one. Of course, considering the shelter is underground, you'll want to be very sure that the soil drains well and that you're not in an area with a chance of flooding.

## Digging the Pit

1. Find a site. As this shelter will be below ground, drainage and safety from vehicles, people or animals potentially passing over your shelter should take utmost priority when picking a site. It's also nice if the soil is easy to dig through, so avoid rocky ground.

2. Measure the outline. Lie down on your back, and using a stick, draw a line on one palm's width away from both sides of your body, starting at your shoulder and moving toward your feet, all the while following your body's outline. Once you have completed this, draw a line to connect the two lines at shoulder-level, thereby creating a roughly triangular shape. If you don't want to follow your body shape and have a bit more room, you can simply create an outline about 7 feet long and 3 feet wide.

3. Dig the pit. Use a small shovel, flat stone or sharp branch to dig the pit about 4 feet deep, following the line you drew on the ground. The excavated soil can be placed around the pit, so as to decrease the actual depth you have to dig. When your pit is complete,

create a 6-inch-wide ledge all the way around it at a depth of approximately 18 inches. If the soils is quite loose (such as with sand) place two long poles onto this ledge on either side of your pit.

## Create your Bedding

1. Set down the bedding branches. Once the pit is dug, line the pit or outlined area with branches crosswise from foot end to head end. These branches do not have to be perfectly straight but should be about 2 inches or so in diameter in order to evenly support the lengthwise layer to come.

2. Stack your branches. Next, lay branches crosswise on top of the first layer. Place the sticks side by side and carefully choose them to fit well together, with no bumps or twigs sticking out, as cushioned by a layer of leaves, you'll be lying directly on top of them.

3. Add the debris. Now, add a 1-foot-thick layer of carefully selected dry debris on top of the latticework to complete your mattress. This is a good opportunity to introduce some ferns (for the nice smell) and beech leaves (to repel insects). Use only the fluffiest and driest of materials (where available) and filter it carefully to avoid twigs, thorns, seed pods and stones.

# Building the Shelter

1. Build the structure. Mentally divide the pit in five equal sections lengthwise. Cover the bottom three fifths with crosswise branches. The branches need to be the correct length so they lie securely on both of the ledges you created, overlapping the ledges by at least 4 inches on both sides. You'll want these branches to be the sturdiest you can find as they'll be carrying debris and soil.

2. Cover the first fifth from the head end. You'll be left with an uncovered fifth near the head end. This will form your entrance to the shelter. You may want to use more branches to reinforce this area and build it up to ground level.

3. Cover and insulate the shelter. Cover the entire structure (minus the entrance) with a 1-foot-thick layer of debris and a 6-inch layer of soil. You should be just above ground level at this point, so use the soil to create a bit of a mound to help rain run off, and add another thin layer of debris to the roof, if you wish, to blend the top layer into the surrounding area to decrease the visual impact.

4. Create the door. The challenge now is to create a sturdy, rainproof (where required) door. You could latch a frame together to fit or use large sections of bark. Fixing the roots of a dug-up small shrub to the door with string can provide a convenient handle.

This shelter is usually more than comfortable enough to sleep in without the aid of a sleeping bag or pad, though don't be surprised if you find yourself having odd, "buried alive" dreams for the first few nights until you get used to sleeping in a small subterranean shelter. I have always enjoyed the low visibility and security this shelter offers, but do want to note that the shelter can really cut you off from the world around you as barely any sound travels through, and little to no light. I have woken up plenty of times only to realize that the day was already in full swing when I opened the door. It's an easy-to-build yet strong shelter that can be readily adapted with more digging to create more space for equipment or even a small fire.

# ✦ ── SNOW SHELTER ── ✦

There are a number of types of snow shelters that can be built, but the one I will describe below is the best example of the various principles at work. It can be adjusted to suit different needs, depending on your circumstances. This design also circumvents the fact that emergency snow shelters are actually faster to build in snowdrifts or banks of snow, as snowdrifts are quite rare in most places. You will essentially be heaping snow in a big pile and hollowing it out. This is important, as very often, snow is not compact or sticky enough to dig out a snow cave. Powdery snow, however, has the amazing ability to solidify once disturbed. Another, more famous alternative involves cutting blocks of frozen snow, but for that technique to be successful, the snow cannot be powdery and some sort of a saw is needed. I have made shelters with snow blocks on several occasions, but never found it quite as convenient as the shelter I will cover here. The shelter below can be made entirely by hand, though bringing a shovel and a saw with you will greatly speed up the process.

## Selecting the Site

1. Mind the dangers. The biggest hazard in relation to being out in the snow is the possibility of avalanches. If you're building the shelter discussed here, you should be selecting level ground but should you decide to dig into a hillside instead, you need to be absolutely sure that your

site is safe from avalanches. Another danger to keep in mind is the cold. Normally, it is fairly straightforward to protect yourself from the cold by wearing adequate clothing; however, when digging a snow shelter, there's a big risk you may be sitting or lying directly on the snow for too long, which will cause the parts of your body in contact with the snow to become cold very rapidly. You also have to look out for snow gathering in your shoes or collecting on your clothes. As you will be quite warm with the exertion of building the shelter, snow may melt on your clothes and make you wet. Snow trapped on your socks, in your shoe will definitely melt. Wear trousers that can be tied around your boot, opt for snow boots designed like the home-made ones I'm wearing in the images and constantly brush snow off your clothes.

2. Prepare the site. Whenever you have picked your shelter location, you may need to create a base as the main room in the shelter, which must be a good 3 feet above ground, so the entrance can angle up from solid ground to the higher floor level of the main room.

## Building the Shelter

1. Create the dome. Place all your belongings in a big pile in the middle of the base (if you had to make one), making sure there are no small, loose items that may become lost. Over this pile of equipment, start piling snow. (Creating this bulk will save you a fair bit of time when it comes to digging out the shelter.) The size of the snow dome you're making can vary according to your own needs, but keep in mind that each of the walls will take a good foot in thickness away from the available space when gauging the size from the outside. The floor level of the shelter should also come out higher than solid ground by a solid 2 to 3 feet, so make your dome 4 feet higher and 2 feet wider than the space you'd like to have inside once it's finished. (More on that later.) For a two-person shelter, a smooth, even dome with a diameter of about 3 to 4 yards and 6 feet of height ought to be

more than sufficient. Once this dome is built, pat it all down well with your hands or a shovel and leave it to sit for approximately 20 minutes. This will give the snow time to "set" and solidify into one large mass.

2. Mark the thickness of the walls. Now, gather about 20 to 30 straight, 1-foot-long sticks. Remove any side branches. Travel around the shelter, and push the sticks straight into the dome (perpendicular to the surface) in random places so that the ends sit flush with the surface. These sticks are going to be your guide as you dig out your shelter.

3. Dig out the shelter. Now comes the fun part. Determine where your entrance is going to be; this entrance should be a good 2 to 3 feet above solid ground and as small as possible, though big enough for you to fit through comfortably and start digging.

Dig in a straight direction toward the center of your dome. If you packed the snow well and it was given enough time to solidify, you should encounter no small collapses while digging.

4. Enlarge your dome. You should find your equipment toward the center. Carefully drag it out through the entrance. Keep digging carefully, slowly enlarging your dome until you reach the tips of the sticks you pushed into the dome. These sticks are an indicator you have reached your target wall thickness of 1 foot. If the day is bright, you may find that as your wall becomes thinner, more blue light will filter in through your walls. This may be a bit unsettling, as it can seem you've nearly dug through the wall, but do not worry. This is why we pushed the twigs into the wall earlier.

5. Finish the ceiling. Create an even dome by smoothing out the surface with your hands so that any melted water will not drip from it.

## Adding an Entrance

1. Now that the dome is complete, place a backpack or other gear up in front of the entrance, blocking it. Pile another big heap of snow in front of the entrance. This pile should stick out from your shelter by about 4 to 5 feet, have a width of about 5 feet and be 1 foot higher than your original entrance, about 6 feet from ground level. You must ensure that this pile is patted down well and forms a seamless bond with the original dome. Once again, collect some 1-foot-long sticks and push them into the sides and roof of the entrance tunnel. This time, the sticks are not intended as a target to reach so much as a way to stop you from accidentally breaching the walls when digging out the entrance.

2. Dig out the entrance. In front of your heap of snow, dig down to solid ground level, or to 2 to 3 feet below the level of your shelter. Make this pit nice and wide, as you'll need plenty of space. The reason for the pit is that cold air sinks while warm air rises. So, by having your main shelter higher than ground level or by creating a big pit outside your shelter,

you'll encourage the cold air from inside your shelter to move there, while the warm air will be retained inside the shelter.

3. Open up the entrance tunnel. After digging this pit (or if you're already at ground level), create a small entrance (with a saw if you have one) by digging at ground level into your entrance, working your way up to the hollow you created earlier. When you reach your backpack or other gear that you used to block the entrance, you can carefully remove it, which should open the entrance tunnel up into the main shelter. Digging here is probably the trickiest part as you're trying to keep the entrance small while digging up a slope. Ideally, the ceiling of your entrance tunnel right at the entrance should be lower than the floor level of the main shelter. You can further improve upon the entrance by building a U-shaped snow wall around the entrance to deflect wind, leaving enough room to get in and out.

## Insulating the Shelter

1. Gather insulation. Now that the shelter is built, you are ready to move in. Gather as much insulation as possible to use as bedding, such as sleeping mats, debris, sleeping bags, spare clothes, etc., applying the principles discussed on page 9 in "Shelter Fundamentals." If you wish, you can shape the snow inside into more comfortable seats, shelves and whatever else you need. Just be sure not to make the wall thinner than the foot indicated by the twigs inserted into the walls.

2. While digging, you probably already noticed that it was quite a bit warmer inside the shelter than outside. If the shelter is small enough, mere body heat may be enough to heat it. Small candles or tea lights can also be used to raise the temperature somewhat. The temperature of the shelter should never be higher than freezing point, but compared to the temperature

*The* Complete Survival Shelters *Handbook*

outside, it should feel like a good improvement. At a temperature of about 30°F, you will probably find that your clothes or sleeping bag are enough to keep you warm and comfortable. Having built such a shelter in −50°F in the Yukon, I can attest that the temperature inside the shelter felt positively balmy and that it was comfortable and cozy enough to spend an extended length of time in!

In the picture below, I have dug away one side in an attempt to show the size better and clarify the different floor levels with the entrance tunnel angling up toward the main shelter.

Again, just like with the other shelters covered, the descriptions are only intended to teach you the underlying principles. Once understood, you should not feel limited by the designs in this book. In the case of snow shelters, for instance, other options may be to simply dig a 3-feet deep hole horizontally into a snowdrift or slope, before digging upward to create a pod big enough for you to sit up or even lie in. Excavated snow can be heaped onto the outside to give you a larger shelter. Another option is to dig a pit, which is then covered by evergreen branches and snow or even just blocks of snow, much like the subterranean shelter we covered earlier.

There are a few considerations to take into account when using a snow shelter. It is very important to not close off the shelter entirely in order to refresh the air. In a snowstorm, for instance, regularly checking the entrance, or even poking an additional hole through the ceiling is very important. I have heard it said that ice formed due to condensation on the inside of the shelter should be scraped away regularly to prevent a decrease in fresh air-circulation, but I have never done so and noticed no adverse effects. In fact, snow shelters, such as igloos are purposefully allowed to build up an ice-layer on the inside as a way to increase structural strength. In any case, feeling drowsy and confused or getting a headache, may be signs that carbon monoxide is building up and more ventilation is needed. In conditions where the weather hovers close to freezing, the benefit of shelter is reduced to only providing shelter from wind (and precipitation); however, the risk is a lot higher, as thawing may cause your shelter to become unstable and collapse.

# IMPROVEMENTS AND BASIC FURNISHING

Many of the shelters covered above are just that: shelters. To actually live in them and increase comfort, you'll want to spend some time improving them and creating "furniture." Many such items do not take much time at all to make and will add a lot of value to your shelter experience.

## Improved Fireplace

A few of the shelters discussed above allow you to have a fire inside. The stacked debris wall shelter even includes a fireplace in its design, while the bent sapling shelter can easily be adjusted to feature a smoke hole.

You will find, though, that having a non-smoky fire inside an enclosed space is trickier than doing so out in the open air. I've always noticed that closing the doorways of these bigger shelters soon lowers the fire and increases smoke production. This is because the heat of the fire pushes large volumes of air outside the shelter through the smoke hole while lesser amounts of fresh air are being drawn in. One way to address this is to create tunnels for fresh air to flow through.

1. Dig a trench. Using a shovel, sharp stone or stick, dig a trench about half a foot deep from the outside of your shelter all the way into the side of your fireplace.

2. Form the tunnel. Cover the trench with small sticks, creating a tunnel. Make sure the tunnel opens from the inside of the fireplace to the outside of your shelter. Cover the sticks with soil. Ideally, this tunnel faces in the direction of the prevailing wind. Some people elect to dig four tunnels, one in each wind direction.

3. Create a funnel. Outside your shelter, you can attempt to create some sort of funnel, which will allow the wind to push more air through. Using a strategically placed stone where the tunnel meets the fireplace, you can regulate the amount of air blowing into your fire. You will find that the fire should burn much more merrily and not be nearly as smoky. On gusty days, though, it's best to nearly close the tunnel over as gusts can cause the fire to spark or hot embers to land outside the fire pit.

## Firewood Storage

I like to store firewood close to the fire to pre-warm it or dry it out if the wood is damp.

You may consider making two storage places, one far from the fire and one close to it. Dried wood can be stacked farther away. When retiring to bed, any wood remaining close to the fire can also be moved farther away for added safety. When using fire inside a shelter, you'll want to ensure that the sticks you're using are not collected off the ground by collecting dead branches still hanging in the trees only. Dead wood lying on the ground for any length of time will likely be full of moisture (causing smoke). You also want to stay away from resinous wood such as fir, pine and spruce, opting instead for broadleaf branches. Wood containing a lot of resin tends to pop and spark a lot. Keeping in mind that you'll be operating a fire in an enclosed space, it's useful to break all firewood into handy 1-foot lengths before storing it inside the shelter. Using thinner branches no more than 2 inches thick will create more heat and light and allow you to control the fire better with less smoke; the downside is that you'll go through your wood fast and will need to pay regular attention to the state of the fire. Thicker "bulk" wood, on the other hand, will last longer, allowing you a slumber here and there, but is harder to keep smoke-free and generally requires the fire to be a bit bigger. I usually keep a mixture available and also ensure a large supply of kindling. Then, when I wake up in the middle of the night with only embers remaining, it is easy to throw some kindling over the top and get things going again.

If you are staying with family/friends and are the person responsible for watching the fire, you could consider wearing one layer less than the others during fireguard duty. This should ensure you wake first when the fire dies down too much, as you'll notice the absence of heat more than the others.

The easiest way to store wood is to create a structure to hold the firewood in place.

1. Create support. Simply hammer two 2-foot long stakes into the ground, about 2 feet apart (or more if you have the space).

2. Create a drying platform. Place two 2-foot long branches parallel on the ground between the two stakes so the wood can sit off the ground.

3. Stack the wood. Place the first layer of wood in a neat row on top of the two parallel sticks between the two upright ones. Stack more wood in the pile until full. Don't store the wood closer than 2 feet from the fire, though, and keep a good eye on it to ensure it doesn't start smoldering.

# Bedding

As became clear with the smaller shelters, providing insulation from the ground itself is very important. When you can afford the time and energy, investing in a good bed is most certainly worthwhile as the more comfortable your sleep, the better rested you are to deal with the challenges of day-to-day life in the wilderness. In small shelters, you will have already built-in a mattress to insulate you from the ground. In larger shelters, you will have to create a more permanent bed. In temperate conditions, you can create a simple bed by forming a rectangular space using a few thick logs held in place with strategically spaced pegs. Fill the rectangle formed by the logs with crisscross branches before heaping dry, fluffy debris on top to the level of the log sides. This is usually more than enough and very comfortable. Every once in a while, you can replace the debris with fresh material.

Using a few fresh fern leaves and beech leaves will keep your bed smelling fresh and insect-free.

In colder climates, I prefer creating the bed by placing logs side by side to the required width. I then like to use narrow sticks to fill the gaps between the logs, and mosses or debris to level the remaining hollows and bumps. A layer of clothes or debris provide adequate padding.

Alternatively, two logs with 4-foot-long, tightly packed branches placed across them can produce a comfortable sleeping place, especially if the sticks are springy.

# Shelving

It is very easy to create a shelf or two inside your larger shelter. This will keep stored items off the ground, where they are less likely to get knocked over. Shelves also prevent items from getting lost in the debris on the ground or in the bedding.

1. To create some simple shelving, jam Y-shaped branches into the ground so that the Y-shape is parallel to the wall. The crooks of the Ys for each branch should be level with each other. In the crooks of the fork, lay a strong branch to connect the two Ys.

2. Jam sticks into the wall at the correct height so that one end of the stick is supported inside the wall and the other end is supported on the branch resting on the forked poles.

3. Place a layer of sticks across these two horizontal sticks to create the surface of the shelf, all the way from the front to the wall.

## Grass Mattress

If you have the time and resources to create one, a grass mattress will really increase your comfort as it can be far superior to a bed made out of leaves. In truth, the mattress can be made out of materials other than grass, such as rosebay willowherb, straw or any other thin and hollow, flexible material.

1. To create the mattress, collect a good two armfuls of 3-foot-long stalks of grass or other material. All the stalks should point in the same direction. You will also need three pieces of cord, each roughly 4 yards in length. Place these three cords parallel on the ground, spaced about 1 foot apart.

2. Grab a handful of grass, split it in half and flip one half over before combining the handful back together. This action will ensure that your bundle has a more even thickness along its entire length.

   Place this bundle across the middle of the parallel cords so that on either side of the bundle, about 2 yards of each cord stick out. One of the cords should be in the center of your bundle, while the remaining two are closer to both ends of your bundle.

3. Use the center cord to tie the grass bundle tightly together by wrapping one end of the cord twice around the other end and pulling tight. You should find that by wrapping the cord twice around itself, rather than the more usual single knot, your knot should create a flat surface on the bundle. Repeat this process with the other two pieces of cord, so that the bundle is tied tightly together in three places.

Ensure that the knots are all on the same side of the bundle, so that the bundle has one flattened side.

4. Grab your next handful of grass, split it once again in half and flip one half over before recombining the bundle. Place this bundle right on top of the previous knots, and tie it down in the same way, using the same flat, twice-wrapped knot you tied the first bundle with. Keep repeating this process until your mattress is the length you wish it to be. You will notice that, because we created a flat knot, the bundles of grass can sit quite tightly together, eliminating any gaps. Once your mattress is complete, you can leave it as is or tidy it up a bit by chopping the ends off the bundles to form more uniform sides, making it easier to move about without it catching on things.

With a bit of care, these mattresses can last a long time and remain incredibly comfortable. Obviously, while producing the mattress, it is easy to make it thicker or thinner, longer or wider depending on your requirements and availability of resources. While the grass is still fresh (and not too brittle) it is possible to roll the mattress up as well. Once the grass dries, though, take caution to prevent breaking the stems.

## Tripod Back Rest

Creating a back rest to allow you to sit in comfort is actually incredibly easy.

1. Gather three sticks, each about 4 feet long and sturdy enough for you to lean against.

2. Tie the sticks together at the top end with cord, cinching between the sticks to allow some maneuverability.

3. Place two of the legs on the ground about 2 feet apart, and place the third leg about 2 feet behind it, creating a triangle. For extra sturdiness, hammer three stakes deep into the ground and anchor the three legs securely to the pegs.

4. Drape a grass mattress over the frame, so that the two front legs of the frame are completely covered by the mattress and there's 1 to 2 feet lying flat on the ground to sit on.

A good sturdy backrest is essential as it allows you to sit in comfort, insulated from the ground, close to the fire. The mattress behind your back will allow heat to be retained and, if placed fortuitously, help block incoming wind.

## Smoking Out Shelters/Cleansing Shelters

Smoking out a living space with acrid herbs is common today in numerous ceremonies and cleansing rituals. However, I have no doubt that the original reason for cleansing a shelter with smoke came from the need to reduce the presence of insects in the shelter. Filling a leaf shelter up with acrid smoke will drive out even the most determined bug.

In order to do this, you will need some form of fireproof container, a fire and materials which smell acrid when heated. Most (fresh) evergreen needles will work well for this, as will sage.

1. Create the fire. In the fireproof container, place a bed of glowing embers from the fire. If you want, you can strengthen the bed of hot coals by adding some small dry branches to it and allowing them to burn up.

2. Create the smoke. Place copious amounts of pine needles or whatever other material you were able to find on top of the embers. Have a means of extinguishing a fire at hand should it all go wrong, though I've not yet seen that happen yet. Once the glowing embers start scorching the material, a thick smoke will be produced.

3. Introduce the smoke into the shelter. At that point, place the fireproof container inside the shelter, and close over most of the entrance. You'll need to keep a visual on the container from outside though, so you can react immediately if you see flames appear. Keep replacing the embers and material regularly, allowing your shelter to be filled with smoke for 30 minutes or so. A good indication that your shelter is truly smoked through is when smoke has begun to seep through the debris walls and roof of your shelter. If you are really keen-eyed, you may notice spiders making a beeline for the nearest exit.

When finished, remove the container, extinguish any remaining embers or material and allow your shelter to air out. This process might have to be repeated every week or so, depending on how many insects are about.

## Making a Tallow Lamp

Most of the shelters described above are gloomy at best, even on the sunniest of days.

Apart from the use of modern lighting such as head torches, candles and lanterns, it can be hard to provide any sort of artificial light inside the shelter. One of the best methods is using oils or tallows. Oils are generally impossible to obtain, but tallows can be produced in a primitive setting. In order to do so, you will need a fire or a camping stove, a fireproof container and animal fat which can be obtained from meat you've hunted or otherwise attained.

1. Gently warm the animal fat in the container over the fire (I used a camping stove). As the fat melts, you will find "fritters" start to form among the liquid fat. Carefully skim these off. Once all the fat has melted, try and skim any remaining impurities out of the liquid or strain the liquid through any cloth you have available.

2. Pour the liquid in open containers. For this purpose you can create clay bowls or use natural, hollow objects such as shells or stones.

3. Insert a wick made out of cord into the fat before it cools. This wick can be lit and will function much like a candle would.

Another material that can be burned to produce light is the resin from evergreens, such as spruce, pine and fir. However, while the light produced is relatively good, the resin burns rapidly and produces a large amount of smoke. The resin also tends to spit while burning, causing a fire hazard. For this reason, such lamps are best used in caves or in an emergency. As an aside, this resin also makes an excellent accelerant for helping you light a fire and, with a few additives, makes a reasonable water-fast glue.

# Living in Primitive Shelters

Living in primitive shelters such as the ones described above is a difficult experience to describe that will depend somewhat on the circumstances.

Many people feel an immense sense of achievement and satisfaction after spending a restful night in relative comfort in a primitive shelter. I've always found the experience of poking at a fire inside a shelter, with stars visible through the smoke hole, to be peaceful and wholesome. The larger shelters especially can induce a sense of timelessness and homeliness with their circular forms and star-shaped roofs. Wandering outside your shelter at night for a toilet break and glancing back at the solid shape with the warm glow of the fire reflecting through the smoke hole and entrance can evoke strong emotions of well-being.

Despite these obviously positive experiences, there are also some potential challenges to consider.

Sleeping in natural shelters may be colder than you're used to. Especially without a blanket or sleeping bag, the lack of their weight on your body may also take some getting used to, even if you are warm. When relying on a fire that must be stoked, your sleep may be interrupted and lighter than usual.

You may also have to get used to visits by the occasional insect or even larger animals. I have come back to my debris shelters in the past to find it inhabited by everything from foxes to rabbits. Once, on a longer absence, I found rabbits had dug a small series of underground tunnels right underneath, with the entrance coming above ground inside the shelter.

Ants like to enter shelters too, and don't seem very disturbed by smoke when smoking out a shelter.

Other annoyances can be the regular trickles of debris falling into the shelter, often finding little gaps between skin and clothes or ending up in your mouth.

Your bedding may be lumpy or noninsulating, requiring a lot of fixing. Debris may be wet or damp or simply uncomfortable.

I have heard it said that if you were uncomfortable in the wilderness, it simply means your skill wasn't good enough, and especially in the case of building shelters, I have always found this to be true. Most of the discomforts described above can be fixed by adjusting your set-up during the day. If you are staying in shelters as a learning experience, I strongly recommend spending multiple nights there in succession. This will allow you to improve your shelter day by day based on your experience during the night. The tricks you'll pick up will prove to be invaluable.

It also means that you should not rely solely on reading a book such as this one. You have to get out there and practice with these shelters. Gain the experience that you'll need to create a good shelter under less-than-ideal circumstances. One of the biggest lessons will be how much energy and time it actually takes to create a useful shelter.

Do not lose sight, though, of the fact that the essence of shelter is to help us survive exposure to the elements. Comfort must come secondary.

A large part of a successful shelter experiences also depends on your mental attitude. You must be content with potential bugs crawling around you in the debris, finding leaves in your underwear and having dirt in your hair. Once you can start feeling more at home in such circumstances and have adjusted your standards to take account of the reality you find yourself in, the experience will quickly improve.

# Chapter 3

# DIY and Modern Material Shelters

Of course, in this modern day and age, it should be very rare to get caught out in the wilderness with truly no equipment. In fact, most of us are able to practice survival skills precisely because the modern equipment we carry allows us to save enough effort and time to build fires and shelters, and learn or practice whatever other skill we wish. From my own experience, most wilderness trips require a blend of using primitive skills and modern camping equipment.

This chapter will focus on modern emergency shelters and basic tarp shelters. If you practiced any of the shelters in Chapter 2, you will have learned how much time you can save by simply bringing a portable shelter. Very often, the principles at play here can easily be morphed with the more primitive techniques described above to get the best from both worlds. I will discuss a number of ideas on combining the modern with the old.

This chapter also covers a number of low-tech shelters you can build at home and take with you wherever you go. I find these shelters particularly interesting, as they can be large and comfortable, yet still relatively lightweight without costing a fortune. Because you choose your own materials, you can make them any color you want and pick those that suit a particular climate. The cost of such mobile shelters is also often much lower than the cost of a store-bought alternative. Building shelters like these and seeing them survive the rigors of the outdoors will boost your own confidence in attempting such projects. You never know, you might even feel confident enough to create a few such shelters for friends and family.

# EMERGENCY SHELTER BAG

The most common ready-made emergency shelter is a simple plastic bag, large enough to contain you, your sleeping bag and pad, and sometimes even gear. These bags are often sold in orange and are aptly marketed as "emergency shelters."

While they pack small, are cheap and expendable, and are undoubtedly handy in an emergency, there are a few downsides you should consider. They are made of non-breathable plastic, so any moisture you generate through perspiration or breathing will be contained in the bag. This will likely leave your sleeping bag damp, if not wet, after a night's sleep. The bag is open-ended at the head end, with no way of closing it. As there are no grommets to allow you to tie the opening to branches or shrubs, it's impossible to set the bag up so that the entrance remains open, yet provides shelter from the rain.

If you are going to spend money, you may as well spend that little bit more and go for a breathable, Gore-Tex bivvy bag instead (more on that on page 131).

This type of emergency shelter works even better in cold weather if you crawl into one with another person, as two people generate relatively more heat than a single person.

1. Setting up your emergency shelter bag is easy: Unfold it, place it on level ground with the opening facing away from incoming weather, slip your pad, bag and gear inside, and crawl in. You can try to use your gear to hold the bag open, while still providing for rain cover for your head.

# REFLECTIVE FOIL BLANKET

Another form of emergency shelter is the reflective foil blanket, also referred to as a space blanket. It is simply a plastic sheet laminated with reflective silver foil on one side. This blanket works by reflecting any heat lost through your clothes back to you. For this reason, it is important to remember that the blanket does not insulate if it is directly touching your body. You need space between the blanket and yourself, which can be created with bulky clothing, a sleeping bag or even debris. If none of these are available, you can try crinkling the blanket as much as possible and loosely draping it over your body. Much like the emergency shelter bag, the materials of the blanket are not breathable, so condensation can form.

This shelter is truly a last-resort emergency shelter and is often used by emergency services when dealing with hypothermia and shock. The advantage are that it packs incredibly small—small enough even to fit in a first aid kit, and is truly marvelous at reflecting heat passed through radiation.

On its own, the reflective foil blanket barely functions as a shelter, and then only in a true emergency. Using it in combination with the debris shelters from the previous chapters, however, will make it a truly formidable piece of gear. You can drape the blanket over the ridgepole of the debris hut on page 25 before adding the rest of the frame to drastically increase heat retention (and cut down on debris falling on top of you). You can also use the blanket to drape the interior of a natural shelter, such as the stacked debris wall (page 37), or use it as a fire reflector, either behind the fire and/or behind your back. The possibilities are truly endless. I heartily recommend carrying a few of these blankets in your equipment.

## BASHA/TARP SHELTERS

Basha is a term which seems to have spread from Australia to the rest of the world. It is a rectangular, waterproof sheet of rubber or plastic, specialized for camping. Bashas have grommets and tying loops in strategic locations, such as along the edges and center. These sheets are usually about 5 by 8 feet. Many of them also come with pop buttons, allowing you to fix two or more together. They are comparable to the pup tents the US Army used to issue to the infantry. Bashas are incredibly useful for creating quick shelters. I always keep a few in my jeep. Even when I'm using a different type of shelter, I will often string a basha up between a few trees to store my gear or provide me with a small "out-of-the-shelter" work area, allowing me to cook or work on projects outside while sheltered from rain or sun.

## Setting Up the Basha

1. Find two to four trees or other improvised uprights to serve as the frame of your shelter. Using cord, tie the basha so that one edge is higher than the other by about 2 feet. Just be sure you don't string it up level, which will cause rainwater to pool.

2. If you want a space for working under, tie it up as high as you can in order to have enough space to stand. If it's only for sleeping under, the lower edge can be pegged to the ground and the higher edge 4 feet off the ground. If the basha has a tying loop, this can be used to pull the sheet up in the center, allowing for less of a pitch or more space underneath. There are really no limits as to how you want to string up your basha to shelter from rain.

## Using a Basha to Collect Water

You can also string up the basha in a way that it collects rainwater for you while keeping you dry.

1. Hang the basha so one corner is lower than the other three.

2. Place a small rock in the center of the sheet, causing a dip. This will gather water toward the center before allowing it to run off to the lower corner.

3. Place a container like a bottle or pan below the drain to capture the water.

## Using a Basha as Shelter from Sunlight

If you would like to create a shelter to protect you from direct sunlight, a basha can serve the purpose, giving you ample shade. Stringing up two bashas one above the other with a couple of inches in between the two also cuts down on the heat being radiated through the material and offers a much cooler experience. Similarly, when using a tent or vehicle as shelter under a hot sun, stringing a basha above it will cut down on the intense heat being generated inside the tent or car. This effect was used very effectively on old "Safari" model Land Rovers, where the manufacturer installed a second roof above the normal roof with a clear gap between the two.

1. Suspend one basha. Find two to four trees or other improvised uprights to be the frame of your shelter. Using cord, tie the basha up so that one edge is higher than the other by about 2 feet if you expect rain. Otherwise string it up so it provides the most possible shade.

*The* Complete Survival Shelters *Handbook*

**2.** Suspend a second basha about 2 inches above the first basha.

When protecting a car roof, tie the basha over the roof bars or use branches as spacers to keep the basha off the roof if your vehicle doesn't have roof bars.

## Using a Basha to Deflect Wind

It is also handy to keep a few tent pegs with your basha, as this will allow you to peg one side of the basha into the ground.

1. Tie one side of the basha to two trees, about 4 to 5 feet above the ground.

2. Stretching the lower edge taut, insert sticks or tent pegs into the ground through the provided holes or loops.

## Using a Basha as a Tent

Alternatively, you can use a length of cord between two trees and peg the basha down on both sides so it resembles a tent.

1. Suspend the ridgeline. Either run a length of cord through loops provided and tie it between two trees, or tie the cord between two trees and drape the basha over it.

2. Insert twigs or pegs into the ground through the holes or loops provided at both of the long sides of the basha, forming a tent. Be sure to keep the basha taut without too many wrinkles.

# MAKE YOUR OWN GROMMETS

If you only have access to a sheet of plastic or a basha where the grommets are threatening to tear loose, wrap the ends of the basha around a small stone and tie a piece of cord tightly around where the material comes together (a bit like a candy wrapper or drawstring pouch) to lock the stone in place. This cord can then be used to tie the basha onto trees or pegs.

## Using a Basha with Natural and Debris Shelters

It makes sense to use a basha in combination with the natural and debris shelters we discussed in the previous chapter. For instance, a basha could be used to roof a stacked debris wall structure or cover a smoke hole when a fire is not in use. Using a basha in this manner can combine the best from both methods of shelter construction or improve on what might have been possible using only one method, while also cutting down on time and energy spent.

# SCANDINAVIAN LAVVU

The tent we're about to build is a very mobile and easy-to-build shelter inspired by the Scandinavian "lavvu." The lavvu is a type of shelter that has been in use by the nomadic Sami people, an ethnic group with an ancestral range covering northern Scandinavia, for hundreds of years. The Sami people traditionally revolve around the herding of reindeer, which have to migrate regularly for food, necessitating a convenient and mobile form of shelter that can withstand the arctic conditions of the far North. The lavvu is similar to a Native American tepee in shape, though is generally a bit smaller in diameter and has a lower pitch to the roof, causing the structure to be quite a bit lower to the ground than a tepee. This lower profile helps keep the structure more stable in fierce winds, which would destabilize a full-size tepee. The lavvu is also round, while the tepee usually has a more elongated form.

The smaller size also means that no special roof poles have to be made and carried around, as the length of poles required can generally quite easily be sourced in the wilderness.

The lavvu we will be describing here is about 13 feet in diameter and 6 feet high in the center. This should give you plenty of space for about 4 people and allow you to have either an open fire or a wood-burning stove in the center.

## Materials

**For the lavvu canvas:**
- 21 yards of fire-resistant and waterproof canvas (I use a 5-foot, 2-inch wide waterproof tent canvas.)
- Scissors
- Pins
- Thread
- Sewing machine
- Measuring tape
- Permanent marker
- Long piece of straight timber
- String

**For the lavvu poles:**
- Three 11-foot poles, about 3 inches thick at the bottom with a fork about 6 inches down from the top (These do not have to be perfectly straight, but should not be longer than intended.)
- Eight 11-foot poles without any forks, about 3 inches thick at the bottom (Again, these do not have to be perfectly straight and can be longer than 11 feet. You can use more poles if you wish. The more poles you use, the more stable your lavvu will be.)

**For the lavvu door:**
- Three slender, straight branches about 1 inch or so thick and 4 to 5 feet long for the door flap
- Buckles and webbing

## Creating the Canvas

Sewing the material together in order to cover the shelter will require the use of a sewing machine. I promise you that it won't hurt to try this, even if you've never used one before. Simply grab a couple of inches of the material you're using and make some practice stitches.

1. Cut and pin bands. Cut three bands of cloth 21 feet long. Lay the first and second band on a flat surface so the first band overlaps the second band lengthwise by about ½ inch. Pin the edges together at regular intervals to hold the two bands together.

2. Roll and repeat. Roll one of the bands up from the longer edge to the pinned edge, and repeat for the other band. You now have two rolls with a pinned edge between them. This makes it easier to feed through the sewing machine.

3. Sew the first seam. Place the pinned cloth on the sewing machine and run a line of large stitches through the middle of the overlapping seam, or ¼-inch away from the visible edge of the band, all the way from the top to the bottom, fixing the two bands of cloth together. You can remove your pins as you pass them. The stitch can be quite large, because it is only temporary and non-load-bearing.

4. Hide your seams. Once finished with this seam, place the two bands on a flat surface and fold the seam over itself so that the sewn edges are both hidden away within the fold. You want to do this neatly so you end up with a half-inch wide "strip" of 4 layers of cloth along the entire seam.

5. Re-sew the seam. Pin the new seam in place and roll the material back up the same way you did before. Place it back into the sewing machine and sew one line of neat and small stitches about ⅛-inch away from the left edge of the folded seam. Repeat this to make a line of stitches to

the right side of the fold so you will have two lines of stitches roughly ¼-inch away from each other. You're going to have to be careful as you'll be going through four layers of material and the stitches have to be strong and they will be visible.

6. Attach the third band. Once you have finished with the seam, remove the canvas from the sewing machine and attach the third band to the rectangle in the same manner (following steps 1 to 5) so you end up with a large rectangle roughly 21 x 15 feet.

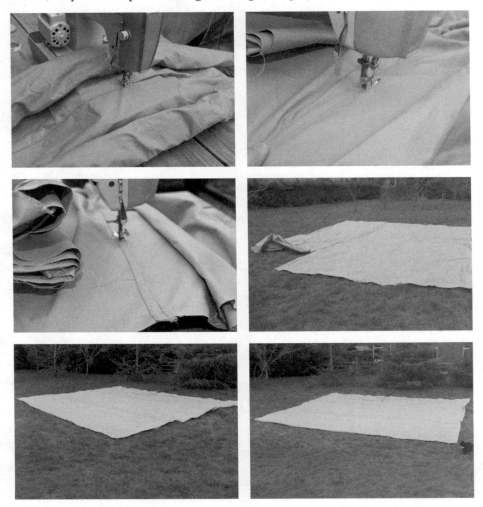

## Measure and Mark the Canvas

1. Measure and mark. Place the cloth on a flat surface. You're going to be measuring and drawing now, which will require standing on the cloth, so if you don't want to mark it (besides

with the pen), wear clean shoes or take them off. Stand along the longer edge (21 feet) of the rectangle running from "left" to "right" of the canvas. Make a small mark along the bottom and top edges of the rectangle, exactly in the middle of the edge, or 10½ feet from either the right or left side.

2. Mark the center of the smoke-hole. Use a long piece of straight timber and lay it across the center of the canvas so that it aligns with the top and bottom marks, essentially dividing the rectangle in half. Measure along this timber 10½ feet from the bottom (where you were standing during step 1) and mark the spot clearly with a large X. This marks the center of the smoke hole and will be the mark used for all the other measurements.

3. Attach a measuring string. For the next step, you'll need a piece of string at least 12 feet long. Tie one end of the string around a marker. Measure out 10½ feet on the string between the marker and the other end. Fix the end of the string in place right on the X-mark using a peg into the ground, or use a helper to hold it in place. If you did a good measuring job, then the marker should now just about reach both the side edges and the bottom edge. If not, adjust the length of the string.

4. Mark the outline. Once it is the correct length, carefully and gently run the marker from the top edge to the bottom on the left, and back up to the top on the right until the lines hit the top edge of the cloth. You should end up with a large C on its side. Leave the string in place for now. The spots where the line touches the top edge should be approximately 1½ feet away from the side edges. With a piece of paper, label one of these spots A and the other B.

5. Make the smoke hole. Shorten the string so the marker is now 1½ feet away from the X and draw a circle around the X. The circle should be 3 feet in diameter. This circle will form the smoke hole.

6. Mark the cut-away. We have too much canvas to create the conical shape so we're going to have to remove some. Place a straight piece of timber from the center X to A and draw a line. Next lay the timber from X to B and draw a second line. Later on, we will cut out the resulting triangle.

7. Draw your doorway. Now move back to the bottom edge, and from that initial halfway mark you made, make a mark 1½ feet to the left, and a second one to the right. This will give you the bottom of a 3-foot-wide doorway. Mark the left side C and the right side D with paper. Place the straight piece of timber so it connects the center X with C. Measure 5 feet up (or more or less depending on how big you want your doorway to be) from point C and draw a line. Place the timber along X and D and measure out 5 feet again (or whatever length you had chosen for point C) and draw the second line. Connect the top of the two lines together with one line parallel to the bottom edge to form the top of the doorway.

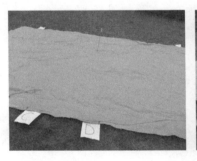

8. Now that all the lines are drawn, cut out the pattern we've created with scissors. Keep the cutouts for later use.

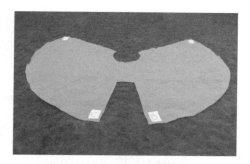

## Sew the Canvas

1. Pin the canvas together. You will now sew the two edges (running from each corner to the smoke-hole) together to form a conical canvas. Fold both the left and right side over so they meet in the middle and overlap by ½ inch. Pin the overlap in place.

2. Make the seams. Place the pinned seam in the sewing machine and stitch the seam the same as before by first sewing a line from top to bottom with a long stitch, then folding the seam over on itself and running two long lines of neat, small stitches from top to bottom.

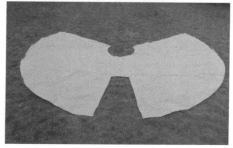

3. Hem the edges. Now that we have the basic shape, we can extend its durability with the little extra effort of hemming all the edges. Simply go around the long circular edge and fold the canvas over twice so you have a ½-inch-wide, three-layer thick "band" running along the entire edge. For the inner edges, such as the smoke hole and doorway, it's best to use some edging ribbon to sew over the edge. Instead of ribbon, you could cut the leftover material into 1½-inch-wide strips to do this too, but then you'll have to wait until after we've created the door flap, which is the next step, as you will need the leftover material to do so.

## Making the Door

1. **Cut and hem the door flap.** From the big, triangular leftover piece that originated from the top edge, create the door flap. If you deviated from my door measurements, you're going to have to adjust things a little, but if not, then measure out a trapezoid shape where the bottom is 4 feet wide, the sides 5½ feet long and the top 2½ feet wide. Hem all but the top using the double fold we used around the bottom edge of our tent canvas.

2. **Cut out strips for channels.** To prevent the door flap from falling through the doorway, you need to create three horizontal channels into your door flap for pushing sticks through. (An alternative is to sew two zippers from top to bottom on both sides of the doorway to allow you to close the door. If you intend to do this, give a bit of thought as to how you place the zippers so that the door flap overlaps the zippers by a good 2 inches on both sides to prevent water ingress.) These sticks will help the canvas door lie flat over the entrance. With more of the excess canvas, cut three 6-inch-wide strips with a length of 4 feet, 1 inch. Take the first strip and center it along the bottom edge of your trapezoid door. You will notice that the strip sticks out by an inch or so on both sides of the door as the strips are purposefully longer than the door is wide. Hem each end ½ inch so they line up with the side of the door flap.

3. Create your first channel. Next, place the strip back on the inside of the door flap so that the two folded-over edges are visible and the strip lies about ½ inch above the seam along the bottom edge of the door. Pin it in place and sew the bottom edge. Now, fold the strip up so that the seam is hidden and fold under the last ½ inch of the top edge and pin it in place onto the door, about 3 inches above the first seam. Sew a line of stitches along that fold too. You should now have a channel you can push a straight stick through once the lavvu is erected.

4. Create two more channels. Repeat step 3 to create two more channels up toward the top of the door flap, each 1 foot or so apart from the others.

5. Position the door flap. Lay the lavvu canvas so the doorway is flat on the ground, and then lay the door flap over the doorway, so the bottom of the door flap lines up with the bottom of the canvas and the door flap is perfectly centered over the doorway. At the top of the door flap, fold under the last ½ inch of the edge and carefully pin it to the canvas.

6. Attach the door to the canvas. Carefully lift the canvas and door flap and sew a double line of neat stitches to fix the door flap to the lavvu canvas. As

an extra option, you can sew in some string here, too, which will allow you to tie the doorway open. I used some webbing straps and buckles for this purpose in the photographs.

7. Enhance the canvas. Though it's not necessarily required, you can now sew loops to the bottom edge of the canvas at regular intervals to allow you to fix the canvas in place to the ground with tent pegs. I have generally found the canvas to be heavy enough to not need this. Another alternative is creating "pockets" for the poles to sit in. This will help stabilize your lavvu and also means you won't have to use pegs. If you want to create such pockets, you'll first need to set the lavvu up and decide on how many poles you will end up using and where these poles will sit, so you can mark the correct spots.

## Procuring Lavvu Poles

The canvas is now ready for use. The original idea, as practiced by the Sami, is to simply pack the canvas and cut new poles whenever the camp moves to a new area. In your situation, this would mean that the canvas could only be used where suitable poles may be found, so depending on the area where you live or your intended use, you may choose to make poles to take along with your canvas.

There is quite a bit of flexibility regarding the poles. They should not be too long as that would cause a gap between the canvas and ground, but they can easily be shorter than intended. In that case, the bottom of the canvas would simply bunch up on the ground. As noted on the materials list above, the poles do not have to be perfectly straight.

When procuring poles, keep the environment in mind and avoid unnecessary destruction of habitat, especially if you're sourcing poles each time you take the lavvu out. You should consider sticking to deadfall or cutting live poles only where you help remedy overcrowding.

## Setting Up the Lavvu

1. Raise the first three poles. To set up the lavvu, slide two of the forked poles through the smoke hole while the canvas is lying on its side with the lower edge bunched up. Lay the poles so their feet are 10 feet apart. Then, reach underneath the canvas with the fork of the third pole and raise the forked side of the two poles up while making sure the two forks are interlinked. When the poles are raised as far as they will go, interlink the third forked pole with the other two, and push the three forks farther up until you can place the third pole on the ground to form a tripod.

2. Add the rest of the poles. Drag the other poles into the structure and slide them up through the smoke hole, placing their tops over the forked poles with three (or more) poles in each space between the forked ones. (The only exception is the doorway, where you'll only use two poles, one on each side of the doorway.) Space their bottom ends out to form a circle roughly 10 feet in diameter. At this point, straighten out your canvas so it is draped equally around the structure.

3. Shape the lavvu. Now, starting with the third forked pole, you can carefully go around the lavvu, moving each pole 1 foot or so outward. As you go around, you should feel the canvas getting tauter. While you're going around, you may have to occasionally push up the smoke hole opening somewhat if it's restricting the outward movement of the poles. Also try to ensure that the doorway is left clear of poles. You are finished moving the poles outward once the lavvu forms a circular footprint on the ground and the canvas is nice and taut all the way around. If you find a few saggy areas here and there due to the crookedness or flexibility of the poles, then that's nothing to worry about. If you created loops for pegs, then you can now peg the canvas down to the ground. Slide the three straight branches through the tubes you made in the door flap, making sure the door flap is outside the lavvu as you do this, and your lavvu is ready for use.

This is a good time to decide whether you are happy with the lavvu as is, or if you wish to add loops for pegs or

pockets for holding the poles. If you do, then you should either mark out where the poles are, or mark where you'd like to attach loops for tent pegs.

The way I described setting up the lavvu is simply the easiest way to put it into words. Once you gain a bit of experience yourself setting it up, you will probably find a method that suits you better. It shouldn't take longer than 15 minutes or so to set up the finished lavvu from start to finish. Taking it down is accomplished by following the set-up instructions in reverse.

## Using the Lavvu

Now that the lavvu is set up, you should find yourself with a circular space that's 13 to 14 feet in diameter. Personally, I like arranging my life around an open fire in the middle, generally keeping the (well-contained) fire between the entrance and my bedding. It is also possible to arrange for a wood-burning stove in the center, though you may have to provide for room around the stovepipe to ensure the canvas and wood stay well clear. An alternative is to use special canvas designed to be in contact with stovepipes and creating a special stovepipe hole somewhere else in the roof. The back wall would be a sensible place, though adequate distance between wall and stove must be maintained.

The lavvu is so simple to make and easy to set up, I wonder why it is not a more popular structure for modern-day camping and events. Of course, throughout history, the style has been immensely popular, being used with local variations by peoples all across the globe. If you're handy, you can even set up a similar structure with bare poles and wrap a plastic tarpaulin around it instead of a shaped canvas. In this book, I also describe the building of a Mongolian-style ger (also known as a yurt). The lavvu is much simpler to make, and when compared to the ger; its only disadvantage is a smaller amount of usable space as the roof goes all the way down to the ground (while the ger has upright walls). For the above reasons, the lavvu is more useful when you are on the move and need shelter for shorter periods of time.

The lavvu design also lends itself well to adaptations in size. You can simply create a smaller lavvu by using smaller poles.

Staying in the lavvu is a simple delight. Its simplicity and the implicit connection to older cultures across the globe make it a special shelter to stay in. I also really like the regularity the poles provide. The structure is one of the most stable I have experienced during inclement weather. I have never seen one blown over, and have seen a lavvu stand proud during a particularly windy storm where a ger ended up with a lean and a few fallen roof poles.

# GER/YURT

One of my favorite shelters is the Mongolian yurt, which is strictly speaking called a "ger" or gher, yurt being a Russian word. These shelters have been used for millennia by the nomadic herders on the steppe land straddling Mongolia and parts of Russia and China. They are very mobile, being easy to take down and transport, yet provide an extremely comfortable home, protecting the inhabitants from the frigid, windswept climate of the area. The design I will describe below is somewhat simplified for Western use and less extreme climates. I have also had to take into account the availability of materials from the hardware store. For instance, traditional gers are covered with a thick horsehair felt cover, followed by a waterproof canvas. In this case, I will dispense with the felt cover, because it likely isn't needed as much in your climes and is in any case very difficult to get.

Looking on the Internet, you will find traditional or modern manufactured gers available for prices ranging from $4,000 to $10,000 and above. Keep in mind that such manufactured gers are usually designed to exacting specifications, are extremely long-lasting and range in intended use, from light camping to serving as comfortable permanent homes. For our purposes, we need a ger that's light and mobile, can be used for a few days or even over a period lasting weeks or months in the outdoors and keeps you well sheltered. With a bit of digging around, it should be possible to produce a good personal ger for about $500 or thereabouts. The example I built for the purpose of the photographs in this book cost me $260 in canvas, $340 in wood (ash wood, which is more expensive than spruce or pine timber, but stronger) and $100 in random materials. The design below is by no means the only way to build one of these shelters. Again, once you understand the principle, you can build it in many different ways.

## Materials

The size of the ger is going to be roughly 15 feet in diameter, which will allow you plenty of living space, even with a family. The ger can be heated with a wood-burning stove or even an open fire provided a large enough smoke hole is made. A large number of steps require the use of power tools or otherwise sharp and potentially dangerous tools. Be sure to wear appropriate and adequate protection such as safety goggles and gloves.

When choosing materials, pick the lightest, yet strongest wood available with a minimum of knots. I used ash for the wall slats and roof poles. Ash is superior but also more expensive. Spruce or pine can be half the price and still provide decent quality. I used spruce to make the doorframe.

You will need:

- 108 wood slats 6½ feet long, no more than ½ inch thick and about 1 inch wide (for the walls)
- 52 wood poles 8 feet long, 1 inch thick and 1 inch wide (for the roof)
- 11 yards of timber, ½ inch thick and 5 inches wide (for the doorframe)
- 100 yards of strong nylon webbing, 1 inch wide (You can also use strong rope instead for wrapping around the walls as tension bands.)
- 60 yards of strong nylon cord ⅛ inch in diameter (for fixing the wall slats together)
- 40 yards 5-foot, 6-inch water-, fire- and rot-proof cloth (or enough 12-ounce water- and mold-treated canvas to cover a conical roof 5 yards in diameter, 5 feet high and about 17 yards in length
- 2 sheets of 6 feet long, 1 inch thick and 3 feet wide treated plywood or alternatively, a metal strip and metal tubing, 7 feet long, 1 inch thick (for the roof ring)
- 6 plate tie rings with rings at least 1 inch in diameter
- drill and about 80 3-inch-long screws
- sanding machine, sandpaper
- varnish, paint (optional)
- wood glue
- hand saw
- sewing machine
- 2 or more clamps

- surform tool
- sharp knife or wood file

## Creating the Walls

Start with the walls, called "khana." The walls will actually consist of three trellises and a door. The lattice design allows the wall to be collapsed in a scissor-like fashion. This design will give you three lattice walls, each measuring about 18 x 5 feet when set up and just 2 x 7 feet when folded for transport or storage. These walls will then be combined with the door to form a circular wall. On the right is an image of a finished section of wall lattice to show you what you are working toward.

1. Mark and drill holes. To start, drill holes into the slats to allow you to tie them together. Place a mark 2½ inches from one end of the slat. (This will become the top of the wall.) Then, place a mark 10½ inches below the first mark. Place six more marks on the slat, all spaced out at the same 10½ inches. This should give you eight equally spaced marks, the lowest mark being roughly 1 inch from the bottom. Drill the eight holes. Use a sharp drill and drill carefully to ensure there's no splinters blocking the holes later. Repeat this for all 108 slats. If you have a drill press, you can stack quite a few on top of each other to speed things up, using a drilled slat as the template. If you are using a handheld drill, how many slats you can do at one time depends on how well you can drill perfectly vertical.

2. Double the holes in half the slats. Divide the slats in half, and set half of them aside. With the rest, drill a second hole 1½ inches above each existing one.

3. Sand and varnish the slats. Now that you have 108 slats drilled with holes, you can spend the extra effort sanding them, rounding the top and bottom,

varnishing or painting them if you wish. If you use a good varnish, stain or paint, you may extend the life of the trellis walls. Having said that, the ger I use for my wilderness courses has untreated spruce slats, and I have not yet spotted any rot or decay. This is probably due to the fact that the slats can always dry out well if wet as they are well-ventilated at all times, and the occasional, unintended plume of wood smoke that fills the shelter will coat the wood.

4. Split the slats in different piles. Remove the weakest six 8-hole slats and six 16-hole slats and set aside. Divide the remaining slats in three equal piles of 16 8-hole slats and 16 16-hole slats per pile. One pile for each section of the wall.

5. Fix slats together. Start making the first section from one of the piles by laying one slat with 16 holes diagonal on the ground, from bottom-left to top-right. Place an 8-hole slat in a crosswise fashion so that the original holes (the bottom holes if it is a 16-hole slat) in both slats are lined up with each other, with the extra hole in the bottom slat just about visible to the top right. This second slat is pointing from top-left to bottom-right. Cut an 11-inch piece of nylon cord and briefly melt the ends to prevent fraying. Poke the piece of nylon cord through the lined-up holes and feed it back through the extra hole in the bottom slat. Tie the two ends of the cord together at the front with a double knot. Your knot should be strong and not come undone. You might even triple-knot it for extra security.

6. Once you confirm that a cord length of 11 inches works for you, you may as well go ahead and cut a whole bunch. In total you'll likely need nearly 900 pieces! Using a candle, you should melt each edge somewhat to prevent fraying.

7. You should now have an upside-down V lying on the ground. Grab a third 16-hole slat, and slide it underneath the second slat so that the second hole in the first slat lines up with the second original hole in this new slat. This new slat should be lying parallel with the second slat. Tie it in place the same way as before. Make sure

*The Complete Survival Shelters Handbook*

that all future slats follow the same pattern; all bottom slats have 16 holes and go from bottom-left to top-right, while all top slats have 8 holes and go from bottom-right to top-left.

8. The next slat gets placed underneath the first one and tied at the third hole, etc. Keep on going until each hole in that second slat has a crosswise piece affixed to it. Since you have 8 holes, it should take you 8 top slats to get to the bottom hole of the second slat. You should now be able to visualize the top of the wall with 8 slats lying parallel on the ground pointing from bottom-left to top-right with one crosswise slat lying on top, joining them all together. You now have the beginnings of the wall; it's time to give this section an end on the right, so that when the wall is standing upright, the ends are aligned vertically. Moving to the right for the moment, tie four more (8-hole) slats in place parallel to the second slat. They should be pointing from bottom-right to top-left. The original top holes in the bottom slats should always be joined to top holes in the top slats. At this point, the top of the right bottom slat and the bottom of the right top slat will show you the extent of your wall toward the right.

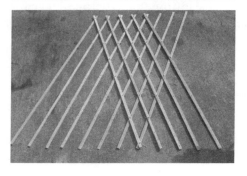

9. Finish the right end of the wall section. Now is the time to start using slats from your reject pile. Select one 16-hole slat. Counting from the bottom of the slat, saw it off about 3 inches above the seventh original hole, tie it in place moving toward the right, pointing from bottom-left to top-right. Saw off a second slat 3 inches from the fifth original hole, and tie it in place to the right of the previous one. Take a third slat, and again, counting from the bottom, saw it off 3 inches above the third original hole, and tie it in place. This completes the bottom slats. Select one 8-hole slat from your reject pile, and counting from the top this time, saw the slat off about 3 inches below the sixth hole and tie it in place from top-left to bottom-right. You will notice that the bottom hole intersects nicely with the last three-hole slat lying on the ground. Now, take another 8-hole slat, and counting from the top, saw it off 3 inches below the fourth hole

and tie it in place. Now take a third slat and saw it off 3 inches below the second hole and tie it in place. This should finish your wall off nicely to the right.

10. Now that you start seeing the pattern, you can tie them together in any order you wish moving to the left. To make life easier, you can lay out the 16-hole slats remaining in the pile in advance. You will want to finish with the last full slats in such a way that the last full bottom slat is joined with the last full top slat at the fourth hole when counting from the top.

11. Finish the left end of the wall section. End the wall by selecting three 8-hole slats from the reject pile. Saw the first one off 3 inches above the seventh hole, counting from the bottom of the slat, and tie it in place from bottom-right to top-left. Saw the next one above the fifth hole and tie in place and the third above the third hole. Select a fourth 16-hole slat from the reject pile, and cut it off 3 inches below the sixth original hole and tie it in place. Now take the longest of the off-cuts, and saw it off below the fourth original hole and tie it in place, and a last one sawn off below the second hole and tie it in place.

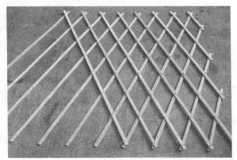

12. Repeat steps 5 to 10 for the other two piles. These three walls will be joined together when setting up the ger so they overlap slightly.

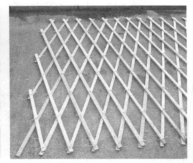

*The* **Complete Survival Shelters** *Handbook*

# Making the Doorway

To complete the wall, we now need to create the doorway, which will be tied between the wall sections to complete the full circle. You can create this doorway any way you wish, but below, I will describe a most simple one.

First we need four 4- and 5-foot pieces of timber, about ½-inch thick and 4 inches wide. These pieces can be cut from the 11 yards of timber listed in the materials section.

1. Create an L-shape. Join two 5-foot pieces of timber together with screws to form an L-shape. Repeat with the other two 5-foot pieces. These two L-shaped corners will form the door posts. The narrower side faces inward, while the wider side faces to the back of the doorway (into the future ger).

2. Complete the rectangle. Attach one of the 4-foot pieces of timber to the bottom of both door posts, joining the two pieces together using long screws. If you use very soft wood, pre-drilling the holes may help prevent splitting. Do the same for the top so you are left with a sturdy rectangular door.

3. Create a lip on the door. Now, prepare the top of the door to receive roof poles. First, create a "lip" by attaching one of the 4-foot pieces of timber to the top at the front of the doorway with screws.

4. Cut 4 notches to hold the poles. On the last piece of 4-foot-long timber, cut four 1-inch-wide notches, pentagon in shape with parallel lines about ½ inch deep, the first one 2 inches from the end, and the other 3 separated by 1 foot from each other, which ought to leave you with 2 inches left.

5. Attach the notched timber. Fix the timber with the 4 equally spaced notches alongside the lip we created in step 3 with screws. They don't have to

sit adjoining, so, somewhere in the center will do fine. This will give you a frame for the roof poles to sit in above the door.

6. Attach tie-rings. At this point, you want to fix 3 plate tie rings in each side of the doorway, facing outward. For extra strength, I use bolts. Position them as follows: the first, 3 inches below the top, a second about halfway up the door, and a third 3 inches above the bottom of the door. Repeat for the other side of the door.

## Setting Up the Wall

Believe it or not, after all that work, you are finally ready to set up your wall for the first time. Pick a wind-free day to do so. Once you gain a bit of experience, you'll be able to set up the ger during windy conditions too.

1. Prepare the layout. On the ground, trace a circle roughly 15 feet across in your mind's eye. Lay the door with the bottom on the imaginary circle, facing out; lay the three (still-folded-up) walls out in a similar manner with the bottoms on the imaginary circle.

2. Raise the wall. At this point, lift one of the walls and unfold it, so it covers roughly a third of the circumference of the circle. You'll find that curving the lattice wall to follow the circle allows it to stay upright by itself. Now, repeat the procedure with the second wall. Place it so that the first wall and the second wall overlap in such a way that the top joints (where the roof

poles will lie) appear to be continuous. Join the sections of wall together with 2-yard pieces of webbing so any overlapping pieces of wall are joined together. Repeat for the third wall. Be sure to leave 4 feet or so where the door lies. When all is secured, you get to move things around a little, so the wall is nice and round with an even height, which should be the same as the door, roughly 5 feet. When you're happy, raise the door, and place the lattice work of one section inside the corner where the plated tie rings are. Tie the lattice to the door using a 3-yard piece of webbing.

Repeat this for the other side of the door. You should now have one continuous circle with a doorway. It may at first be a little fiddly to set the walls and door up properly, but after a bit of experience, it'll become second nature.

3. Attach the tension band. At this point, tie one end of an 18-yard rope or webbing strap to the top plated tie ring in the doorframe, and walk it around the top of your wall to the other side of your door. Tie it off there. You'll want to make sure that this rope sits nice and level and fits the circle snugly as it will form the tension rope against which the entire weight of the roof will push. You can help keep it level by flipping the rope over one in every four or five diagonal slats.

Your walls should now enclose a space roughly 15 feet across. The flexibility of the ger means you can make it slightly larger (lower, with less roof pitch) or slightly smaller (higher, with a bigger roof pitch). This flexibility also allows you to put it up on less-than-flat ground, as you'll be able to compensate by having parts of the wall slightly less expanded.

# Making the Roof Ring

Now that the walls are raised, it's time to build the roof of the ger. The central part of the roof, and the most important, is the roof ring, often referred to as the smoke hole. The official term is the "tono." Again, there are hundreds of ways to build one. I will describe one in-depth, a wooden one anyone can make, and another one, made out of metal, more briefly for those of you with basic welding skills.

1. Count the roof poles needed. Some people lay one over every top joint in the wall as well as the notches we made in the top of the doorway, while others prefer to lose a little weight and use one pole for every two joints. I alternate between both, depending on what weather I am expecting. With that in mind, I count a potential for 52 roof poles for the roof of the ger being described here. The roof ring is going to have to be manufactured in such a way that it'll support exactly the same number of roof poles.

2. Draw the roof rings onto wood. To start, organize yourself enough 1-inch-thick sheets of plywood to contain five 3-foot, circular shapes. Get a nail and a pen, and tie them together with a bit of string so there are 18 inches of string between the two. Hammer the nail into the board at the point where the center of the circle will be. To conserve wood, do it in such a way that the pen will just about reach the edges of the board. With the pen, draw a circle. Retie the string, leaving the nail in place, so instead of 18 inches, the string measures 12 inches between nail and pen. Draw a second circle inside the original one.

3. Saw out the roof rings. Drill a hole big enough to hold your electric saw blade on the inside of the inner circle. Using a saw capable of rounding corners, follow both circles. You should now hold a ring in your hand which has an overall diameter of 3 feet, and an inner diameter of 2 feet. Place this ring on another part of the sheet of plywood, and trace both edges again before sawing it out so you have two identical circles. Repeat this process 3 more times to create five identical circles.

4. Glue the circles together. You should use a strong wood glue that can withstand damp or wet conditions. Clamp the rings down as tight as you can or place a heavy weight on top. When the drying time indicated on the glue bottle has elapsed, remove the roof ring from under the weight.

5. Shape the roof ring and mark the holes. Use a surform tool to shape the roof ring as round as possible, both the outside and inside. Next, measure the circumference, which should be around 113 inches, and divide this by the number of roof poles you intend to use. In my case, with 52 roof poles, the figure is slightly above 2 inches. Decide which side of the roof-ring you'd like to face inside the ger and make marks representing each roof pole along the outer rim of the roof ring approximately 1½ inches above the bottom.

6. Drill the holes. The next step involves using a chisel-style drill bit to drill the 52 holes through the wall of the roof ring where you marked them in step 5. As the poles will be sitting at somewhat of an angle to the surface of the roof ring, you'll

need to drill into the surface at an angle. It's not critical if it's a bit off here and there, so holding the drill at roughly 25 degrees from the horizontal, pointing downward works well enough. If you wish to be a bit more precise, you could lean the ring against the wall at the desired angle and drill straight down instead. You can help accuracy and preserve the sharpness of the more expensive chisel-like drill bits by pre-drilling the holes with a smaller-diameter drill bit. Drill all the holes to a depth of no more than 3 inches, which should be more than enough to hold the roof poles securely.

7. Now that all the holes are drilled, you can use a surform tool or wood file and sandpaper to remove any further imperfections, should you wish. I've even used some wood filler to make the surface perfectly smooth.

8. Finish the roof ring. Once you are happy with the shape, use thin but long screws to fix all the circles together. Be sure not to block any of the holes you drilled by screwing through it and pre-drill holes to prevent splitting where appropriate. After that's done, give the whole circle a few coats of weather-resistant stain or varnish. I have also heard of people who used fiberglass to give the roof ring even more strength and increased protection from the elements. The ring in the photographs was rot-proofed before being painted with a few coats of gloss. I sanded the ring again between each coat to remove any imperfections. It's worth the extra effort as the roof ring will quite literally be in the center of the ger, and the eye is automatically drawn to it by the roof poles.

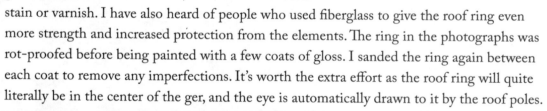

*The* Complete Survival Shelters *Handbook*

# AN ALTERNATIVE ROOF RING

Another method of making this roof ring is by creating a circle out of a 9-foot, 2-inch strip of metal. The holders for the roof poles can be created by getting some metal tubing with an inner diameter of about 1 inch and cutting little 3-inch lengths of tubing off. If you alternate a 25-degree cut with a straight cut, you'll get lengths with one angled and one straight side, meaning that when you weld them onto the circle, you can angle them all down to accommodate the pitch of the roof. When making one of these, you may notice that the ring easily changes shape. Don't worry about that, because once you've welded on the bits of tubing, there will be no flexibility left.

## Making Roof Poles

At this point, we get to cut and shape the roof poles to the correct length.

1. **Shape the poles.** Use a sharp knife or wood file to round off the last 2 inches on one end of each of the 52 poles. This is the end which will be inserted into the roof ring. If you wanted, what you could do now is use a drawknife or something similar and shape the roof poles further along their length. You could also cut little notches around the edges to decorate. Staining, varnishing or painting is also a good option at this point. The poles in the images were carved, sanded and varnished.

2. **Cut the poles.** Remove 4 poles from the pile and set them to the side for the doorway later. Cut the remaining 48 poles to a length of 8 feet, measuring from the rounded end.

3. **Fix loops to the bottom of the 48 cut poles.** Once you are happy with your poles, about 1 inch away from the non-rounded ends (the wall-end), drill a hole. Drill a second hole about 1½ inches from the same end. Thread a 12-inch piece of cord through both holes, and tie it off at

both ends, so a 1½-inch loop is formed on one side. This loop will allow you to hook the pole over the lattice wall to hold it in place.

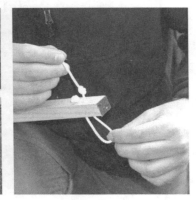

## Constructing the Roof

Before we can measure and cut the poles going from the roof ring to the door, we first need to erect the ger as we have it now. Following the steps in "Setting Up the Wall" on page 98, set up your wall again, and ensure the tension band or webbing strap is securely fastened around the ger to the top plated tie rings on the left and right side of the door.

1. Raise the roof ring. Take three roof poles and place them at equal intervals along the wall. Take the ends of two of them and loop them over the wall, with the rounded end lying on the ground near the center. Grab your roof ring, and bring it inside the circle. Holding the roof ring at the correct angle, count out the empty junctions between the two fastened poles. Count out the same number of gaps on the roof ring, and insert each pole in the space to either side of this gap. Holding the end of the third pole in one hand, lift the roof ring carefully with the other. As you lift it, at some point, you should be able to slide the end of the third pole into the roof ring. You should now be able to push the roof ring up as high as it must go, using the third roof pole only. Count out the gaps on the roof ring between the pole you're holding and the next one along. You should then count out the same number along the spaces at the top of the wall. Once you found the junction where the pole belongs, carefully loop the pole over the wall, and very, very gently, allow the wall to take the weight. Be very careful, as the structure is extremely delicate. There are currently only three poles holding up the roof ring and pushing out on the walls, which are designed to be pushed out equally along

the whole circle, so you can see the danger here. When there is a bit more sag than I'm happy with, I sometimes place a roof pole upright underneath the roof ring to help hold it up while I fit a few more poles.

**2.** Fit more roof poles. If it appears to be holding, carefully lift a fourth pole, and slot it in place somewhere halfway between two poles, making sure that the count is equal at the wall and the roof ring. Keep on going around the structure in this manner until all the poles are in place, except the door poles. Check that they are all seated correctly.

**3.** Fix the poles over the door. You can now place the four leftover poles in the spare slots in the roof ring and lay them across the door, roughly lining up with your notches. Mark them 1 through to 4. Mark the notches the same way and draw a line on the poles where they should be sawn off to correctly fit in the notches. Saw off the ends.

Congratulations! The framework of your ger is now complete! This will probably be your first opportunity to really see the wonderful mix of patterns and lines being created and will give you a feel for what it will be like to camp in. You can see how prominent the roof ring has become, with all the roof poles drawing the eye toward it.

4. Adjust the shape of the ger. Make sure that the bottom of the wall follows the same circle as the top of the wall. Sometimes, the ger may "lean" a little to one side, or have more of a muffin/cupcake shape. If this is the case, carefully move the bottom of the wall out a bit in the right locations. If there's a lean, or if the roof ring isn't horizontal, you can gently push the ger so it stands straight or use a roof pole to nudge the roof ring straight. If you feel that there's not enough of a pitch to the roof, then you can shorten the original tension band. One way to do this is to temporarily tie a second tension band around the ger, tightening it so you have the shape you are looking for, and then re-tying the original tension band in place before removing the temporary one. Warning: Never remove the tension band while the roof is in place before replacing it with another one!

5. Make your knots permanent. If everything is working correctly and looking good, you should take the opportunity to use a liberal amount of some strong, fast-drying glue to soak all the knots that you made. This will help prevent the knots from becoming undone over time. An alternative to glue is silicone. Do not forget the knots on the roof poles. While the framework is standing, pace out (or measure) the inner diameter of your shelter at the ground in several directions. You'll want these measurements in the next step.

## Creating the Roof Canvas

Now we will turn our attention to the canvas cover for the roof and sides. There is a wide variety of materials available for you to choose from, from water-, fire- and rot-proof heavy canvas and plastic-laminated cloth to more modern tent fabrics. If you plan on using the lighter tent fabrics, you need to consider that it will be noisier on windy days and that you either should not have an open fire/wood-burning stove inside, or use fire-resistant canvas for at least the first yard surrounding the roof ring. Even so, there's always a risk when mixing fire with modern tent fabrics. Old fashioned cotton tent canvas, unless it's waxed, will leak where it's touched by roof poles or other objects so is not a good choice here. I made the mistake of using it once for a ger and ended up having to silicone the entire roof canvas!

What material you choose, then, really depends on your preferences. I have generally used the heavier-grade water- and fire-proof waxed canvas. The main disadvantage is its bulkiness when packing up the ger and, to some extent, its weight, though generally, you'll be using a vehicle, so weight is less of a concern. Another downside may be that it's much more difficult to sew heavy canvas with a home sewing machine (though very much doable). Most materials are produced on rolls about 5 feet wide, in which case, you'd need approximately 20 yards for the roof and 17 yards for the wall.

1. Transfer the roof to the ground. There are ways to calculate the exact shape and size of the canvas roof, but I prefer instead to shape the canvas to the roof, rather than rely on math. In order to make the measuring and fitting easier, set the roof up on the ground by itself as follows:

   Hammer two strong pegs deeply into the ground, the width of your doorframe. Tie one end of the tension cord to one peg, and the other end to the other. An alternative method is to lay your doorframe on the ground instead of two pegs. Lay the existing tension rope or webbing strap out in a circle, using the measurements or amount of paces you took of the inner diameter in the previous step when gluing the knots. Make sure the rope forms as perfect a circle as you can get, as it represents the circumference of your shelter at roof height. Using the tension rope as a guide, hammer 8 to10 more pegs into the ground at roughly equal spaces, just to the outside of the circle formed by the tension rope. Place the roof ring toward the center of the circle.

2. Raise the roof ring. Take three roof poles, and insert two of them into the roof ring in such a way that the loops at the bottom ends of the two poles end up looped over two of the pegs you hammered into the

ground. Pop the third roof pole into the roof ring, while raising it up, and carefully place the loop at the bottom end of the third pole over the most conveniently placed peg. Just like when you were erecting the roof on top of the wall, the structure ought to stay up, albeit not in a stable manner.

3. Place the remaining roof poles. Using more roof poles, use each hammered-in peg or stake to place another roof pole into the roof ring in the same manner. The handiest way to select the correct hole in the roof ring is to place the pole over the peg and try the most likely hole. If it slides in smoothly, all is good; if the roof ring forces the pole to move away from the peg, select another hole right next to it. Once all pegs are occupied, go around the outside, and carefully place the tension rope or webbing strap over the end of the poles so the poles

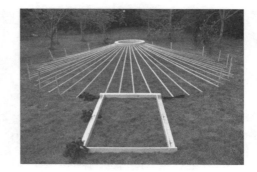

are pushing against it. Fill up the remaining holes in the roof ring by slotting poles in place, ensuring that the back end of the roof poles are kept in place by the tension band. Of course, just like before, you are now left with the gap where the door is meant to be. The easiest way to cover that gap is to lay a plank against the inside on the initial two pegs, and pop the roof poles against it in their correct order. Another option is to slot these 4 roof poles in place, and hammer a peg into the ground at their back end to keep them in place. If it all went smoothly, you should now have a perfectly shaped roof sitting on the ground. Enjoy the view; it's a rare one!

Now that the roof is at a workable height, it should be accessible for fitting the roof canvas over most of its surface. When you need access to the center, you can always remove a couple of poles temporarily to create walking space.

Sewing the material together in order to cover the shelter will require the use of a sewing machine. I promise you that it won't hurt to try this, even if you've never used one before. Simply use a couple of inches of the material you're using and make some practice stitches. When I put my first ger together, I had barely touched a sewing machine. Considering that the ger is still doing well and the stitching strong, yours will be too. Especially as the instructions below should produce far superior seams than my first attempts!

The exact pattern you decide to use is up to you, of course, but for the purposes of this demo ger, I will be laying the canvas on in long bands.

4. Place the first band of canvas. Start at the left side of the roof, and lay a band of canvas over the roof, so that the left side of the canvas overlaps the left side of the circle by 4 inches and the band runs all the way from back to front, ensuring that at the right-most corners of

the band, a good 4 inches is left available outside the roof. You can use clamps to hold the canvas in place correctly. Mark the left side of the band of canvas so it follows the curve of the roof, again ensuring that there are 4 inches left over outside the circle. Cut off the excess.

5. Place the next band alongside the previous one. Make sure, once again, that there are 4 inches of material sticking out over the edge of the roof. You'll also want to align the left edge so that this new band overlaps the previous band by about ½ inch at the minimum. You will find that, due to the curvature of the roof, with the best will in the world, you will not be able to have a constant ½-inch overlap. Instead, if the band is aligned so there's ½ inch of overlap in the middle of the long edge, coming down the roof, the overlap will increase.

6. Pin the bands together. Once the second band is in place, use pins to attach it securely along its entire edge to the previous band. Make sure that all pins are ¼ inch away from the edge of the second band, as this is where you are going to sew the two bands together.

Mark the newly added band again, 4 inches from the edge of the roof, and cut off any excess material.

7. Sew the two bands together. Carefully remove the sheet of material from the roof, and sew the pieces together with stitches as large as your sewing machine can make them and ¼ inch away from the edge. This should also be the line that your pins follow. Pull out your pins as you come along them. Rolling up the material which is to travel through the sewing machine is a great help if you're sewing heavy canvas. You could also place the sewing machine on a skateboard or something comparable to allow the material to lie still and the sewing machine to travel past it. The stitch you're sewing

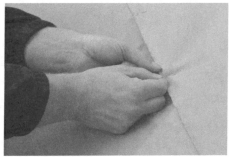

will be hidden inside the real seam and so only serves a temporary function, which is why it can be a bit messy and have large stitches.

8. Once you have finished stitching the two bands together, go back to your roof frame, and place the material back on it, but upside-down. You can now clearly see where the overlap is greater than the ½ inch. Trim the material back so all along the edge, the material only has an overlap of ½ an inch. The cut should also be ¼ inch away from the line you stitched earlier. Flip the material back over into its normal position and fold the seam underneath the right band, and allow the left band to fold underneath the seam. Make sure the fold is neat and as close to the original seam as possible. You should have four layers of cloth in this fold and the fold ought to be around ½ inch wide.

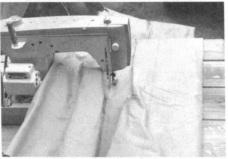

9. While you're folding 2 inches at a time, insert pins to hold the fold in place.

Folding the seam in this manner will allow you to produce a much stronger joint, and also means that water runs off and cannot force its way through the material. As the sewing of the roof progresses, at some point, you're going to have to switch to fold the seam underneath the left band instead. When exactly this happens depends on the width of your bands of material. If in doubt, place the material back onto the frame, and check to see which way you'd need to fold the seam to allow run-off. In any case, when the fold is complete and runs the entire length of the material, place it back on the sewing machine, and run a smaller, neater stitch along the entire length of the left edge of the fold. When finished, run a second one, parallel to the first, along the right edge of the fold. (As the fold is under the material on the

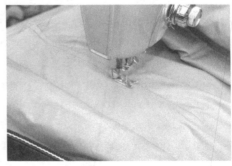

right, you will have to do this by feel and observation of the left stitch. Alternatively, you can flip the canvas upside down.)

Note: As you are sewing through so many layers, if you're using heavy material, you will need a strong sewing machine and a large supply of sharp needles. Change them regularly. Nothing will mess up the stitches more than a blunt needle.

10. Add the next band. If your bands are as wide as mine, you will find that the second band of cloth extends at least somewhat over the roof ring. If not, add a third band of cloth in the same way you added the second one. Once your bands are extended over part of the roof ring, gather any excess material in the roof ring and pin them together.

Make sure that the sewn canvas is placed over the roof frame so that the outer rounded edge overlaps the edge of the roof by the 4 inches we left earlier, and the inner rounded edge overlaps the roof ring by 2 inches. Smooth out the canvas and secure it in place with clamps if needed. Lay the next band of canvas over the right side of the roof so the left edge overlaps the existing canvas by ½ inch near the

roof ring and more near the ends, just like when we placed the second band earlier. Clamp the band in place. When you're happy with how it's lying, tuck the new band underneath the previous bands, so when sewn, the water can run off. Pin the band in place and sew it together using the same method as before. Keep in mind you have to reverse the fold, so the water will run off.

11. Complete the final band. After you have sewn both joints together, place it back on the frame and pin the next band in place. Sew it together, and fit it back over the frame to make sure it fits correctly. Add more bands if necessary.

12. Cut out the roof ring. I cut my cloth to follow the inside of the roof ring. You can seam the edge, or use webbing or other strong material to reinforce the cloth.

**13.** Reassemble the ger frame. Now that the roof cover has mostly been finished, you can remove it from the frame, and disassemble the frame itself. If you still have daylight hours left and are happy to continue sewing, you can set up the entire frame again, starting with the walls. Place the roof cover back over the ger frame, and check that it is nicely centered. You may need to use a stick or pole to help you reach the higher parts of the roof. You will find that it probably fits a little bit differently over the frame due to slight differences in how the roof sits over the frame compared to how it sat on the ground. You'll see that the pitch of the roof is slightly less now, though it shouldn't impact negatively on the fit of the canvas. Make sure your roof cover is perfectly centered; use webbing or rope to tie the canvas in place.

**14.** Finish the roof canvas. Trim off the edge of the canvas so it only extends 4 inches beyond the roof poles.

Where the door is, you will notice that the shape of the canvas is not perfectly rounded. That's okay. Measure the distance from the center of the door all the way around the ger back to the center of the door. In my case this is about 17 yards; for measuring purposes, add 2 feet to your total for a total of 19 yards. Using your off-cuts and leftovers, create a band the length of your calculated number. This band is going to be sewn to the roof cover so it hangs down over the top part of the wall. We want the band to be at least 1 foot wide so that there's plenty of material to fix a rope around it, which will hold it to the frame. This band can be longer than 1 foot in width; the only limitation being the weight and bulk you're allowing your roof cover to be. If your material is light, you can even just fix the whole wall cover to the roof cover into one big cover for the whole ger. In any case, for this example, I am going to have just a short band and keep roof and wall cover separate. Just to be sure that the width of the canvas is enough to reach from the top to the bottom of the wall, measure the height of the wall and the width of the cloth you bought. If you find that your cloth won't quite reach the top of the wall, you'll have to leave more material on the roof canvas, so it will overlap the wall canvas by at least 6 inches. Sew this band onto the roof canvas.

15. Place the canvas back over the roof. It should fit quite loosely. The reason we left the roof cover a bit bigger is to account for possible shrinkage as well as to allow the shape of the ger to differ somewhat as the exact size and shape of the ger will never be precisely the same. When you're happy with the fit, remove or roll up the roof canvas to allow you full access to the wall lattice.

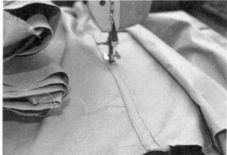

## Making the Wall Canvas

1. Measure the canvas. Using clamps or safety pins, temporarily fit canvas around the ger. You'll want the canvas to start at the right side of the door and travel all the way around the ger to the left side of the door. If you have it to spare, it's wise to leave an extra foot or so in length. Make sure that the bottom of the canvas reaches the ground comfortably, perhaps even with a

couple of inches to spare. When your wall canvas hangs properly with the clamps, cut off any excess, take the cloth down and hem the top and sides to prevent fraying by doubling over the edge twice before stitching it together.

2. Create attachments. Hang the canvas back up using the clamps and use spare webbing to create loops at the top edge. The loops need to be big and long enough to fit over the wall lattice and, once looped on, allow the canvas to hang properly. A loop created out of 3 inches of webbing is usually enough. You shouldn't have to create more than a dozen or so of these loops. Once the loops are in place, you can remove the canvas from the wall and use the sewing machine to liberally stitch the loops to the canvas.

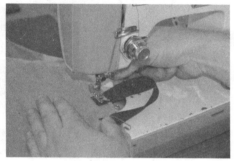

3. Finish the wall canvas. Hang the canvas back in place over the wall for a final fitting. If you wish, you could fashion a method to attach the canvas to the doorframe, but I've never found this necessary. If it all fits as intended, hem the bottom of the canvas by folding a ¼ inch of cloth over twice and sewing the fold together.

## Finishing the Ger

1. Place the roof canvas over the roof, and ensure that it is sitting evenly and overlapping the wall canvas with the foot-wide band. Use the webbing strap we created when measuring the roof canvas and fit it around the top of the wall, just below the bottom end of the roof poles, pinning both the wall and roof canvas in place.

3. Measure two more straps. Measure out two more cords or webbing straps, each of which will be fixed to the plated bottom and middle tie rings at one side of the door, run all the way around the ger, and then be tied at the other end of the doorframe. The

middle one will wrap around the center of the wall to keep the wall cover from blowing about and to allow you to rest your back against the wall. The bottom one will stop the canvas from lifting up with wind and should be about 4 to 6 inches above the ground.

4. Create two roof straps. For high winds, you should also measure two cords which will loop over the roof and be pegged down to the ground. When viewed from the door, the first one will go from the left rear, over the front of the roof, to the right rear, forming a U-shape. The second one will go from the left-front to the right-front, but over the back of the roof. The finished picture below shows the ger with these ropes in place. In high winds, the wind can lift the roof up, much like a plane wing generates lift, before dropping it again and repeating the cycle. This regular up-and-down slamming can damage the roof ring, especially if it is a wooden one. The ropes pegged to the ground will usually be enough to prevent this from happening. In really severe wind, a piece of wood (a strong stick or timber pole will do) can be placed on top of the roof ring with a rope tied tautly between the middle of the piece of wood and a sturdy peg in the ground. Once, during a severe storm, I experienced two or three fallen roof poles with a noticeable lean to the ger the next morning, though I might have been able to do a better job on those anchoring lines and I did not have a rope going from the roof ring to a sturdy peg into the ground.

## Usage and Adaptations

I use the ger described above for extended camping trips, emergency shelter and for teaching courses in. I provide heat and light with an open fire in the center, right underneath the roof ring. The above ger, therefore, is described with this type of use in mind and is as light and basic as possible.

**Door**—For weight-saving purposes, we didn't actually make a door to fit in the frame we created. You could make a nice door to fit if you wish, but with the way I use the ger I have never really needed one. Instead, I have always covered the doorway with a curtain made from the same material as the canvas wall.

**Stove use**—The roof hole is left open to provide plenty of space for smoke to escape through. You could adapt it by integrating "hoops" into the roof ring, over which canvas or clear plastic can be placed. This can be either removable (to provide ventilation) or permanent roof cover. The hoops are there to prevent water from gathering on top of it. You could further adapt such a cover over the roof ring to accept a stovepipe so a wood-burning stove can be used. There is special material available online, usually referred to as a "fireproof flue adapter," which is designed to act like canvas (waterproof and flexible) yet tolerates the heat generated by the stove flue. If this is what you wanted to do, then you'd only have to cover a quarter of the roof ring cover with this material in such a way that the stove flue does not touch any wood, canvas or plastic.

Of course, a wood-burning stove can be placed in other parts of the ger rather than right in the center, provided you keep it at least 3 feet away from the walls and you integrate a fireproof flue adapter as mentioned above.

**Insulation**—The design above also relies on the canvas alone for insulation, and as such really only protects against rain and wind. You could improve upon this by placing space blankets over the frame before tying on the canvas, although this will create a rather surreal look inside the ger. If you found the sewing easy, you could even create a duplicate canvas made out of space blanket material, lined on the outside with thick fleece. In that case, you'd have an inner layer of reflecting material, a mid-layer of insulation, and an outer shell of waterproof canvas. These changes make the fabric of the ger more susceptible to fire damage, so extra care would be needed.

**Windows**—It's relatively easy to use clear plastic to create windows in the canvas, increasing the amount of light available.

I have to confess, I absolutely love taking a ger into the outdoors. There's something about the round shape of the lattice wall and the roof poles converging toward the center that is really pleasing to the eye and induces a relaxed state of mind. Added onto that is the sense of accomplishment in having created such a good shelter by hand from raw materials. On a more practical level, the ger provides a lot of living space, which can be utilized in many different ways. Bedding, seating and work surfaces can easily be accommodated, while temporary shelves and hooks can be fashioned to use the walls themselves for storage. And who doesn't enjoy sitting around an open fire? If you do have an open fire, placing a stick over the roof ring and then suspending a hook from it with a strong rope will allow you to hang pots over the fire for cooking. When I'm teaching courses in the ger, I use a cast-iron Dutch oven to cook stews for all participants in this manner, followed by hot water for dishes.

The ger packs up relatively easily and with practice, can be set up by one person within the space of an hour. When disassembled, the canvas and wooden parts of the ger easily fit on top of most cars equipped with simple roof bars. The canvas can also be stored in the trunk.

# Chapter 4

# Modern Store-Bought Shelters

These days, an enormous number of fabricated shelters for any need or budget are readily available from the store. Rather than covering different makes, models or manufacturers or simply providing reviews that you can find anywhere on the Internet or in magazines, I will focus on different types of modern, store-bought shelters. I will occasionally refer to specific products only to describe certain forms of shelters where I was unable to find generic options. For most of these shelter types where manufacturers are named, there will be other manufacturers who produce similar products. As such, my writing does not imply an endorsement of one brand over another, but simply describes my experiences using the shelter types covered.

Even as an experienced outdoors-person, you may be surprised by some of the shelter options available.

# HIKING TENT

We have come a long way from the heavy ridgepole canvas construction, which required sharing equipment between multiple backpacks and fitting heavy poles in just the right order, never mind regularly recoating waterproofing chemicals. Now, only scout groups and armed forces who have the logistics to carry such heavy tents about will benefit from their undoubted durability. One other circumstance where the heavy canvas tent still rules supreme is in arctic winters, as it is the only tent rigid enough to support heavy snowfall and allow the safe use of a wood-burning stove.

Now, except during winter trips to the Yukon, Siberia or similar destinations, we use lightweight hiking tents with polycotton waterproof material or other advanced fabrics and ultra-light carbon fiber flexible poles. The weight of such tents can easily be absorbed by one person's backpack. The typical tent now also features advanced designs to make full use of flexible tent poles, creating a small, yet comfortable space, often with a built-in awning, allowing work or storage outside the main body of the tent, yet out of any rain.

As for what type of hiking tent works for you, well, that depends on your needs and desires. Do your homework before buying. Read reviews, and when in the shop, check for strong, neat seams. Many cheaper tents come with single-thread seams, which are taped for waterproofing. While taped seams aren't necessarily bad, make sure that the stitching itself is strong and durable. Check the zippers too. They should be sturdy and when closing or opening, should not catch any fabric. Sadly, many tent manufacturers do not pay sufficient heed to their zippers; when they catch tent cloth in their sliders, this can lead to frustration, ripped material, unmatched teeth or stuck sliders.

## Camp Location

When using such a tent, the main thing is to consider the camp location. Take full advantage of shelter that's already present such as trees blocking the wind or overhanging branches taking the sting out of the rain. The site should be safe, close to required resources, ideally flat and relatively soft.

Keep in mind that a tent pitched next to a water source will be soaking in the morning. When picking a site, you also want to ensure that you do not disturb the natural environment too much, so avoid flattening a site yourself or cutting away live branches with abandon where possible. Be sure you are able to erase any trace of your presence when you pack up. If you are using a tent in one site for a longer period, consider moving it every few days to avoid grass or other plant life perishing underneath the tent.

# Tent Anatomy

I picked the generic tent I'll be describing below because its construction and set-up will be similar to most modern tents. And it showcases certain useful features very well.

As with most tents, the flexible poles are threaded through tubing sewn into the tent. With this tent, however, the poles are threaded through the outer tent, which is waterproof. (I also have a tent where the poles are threaded through the inner tent, with the outer tent placed over the top of it.) The advantages of a tent where the poles thread through the outer tent are twofold. First of all, you'll be able to set up the rainproof, outer shell of the tent first, so the inner tent and gear remain dry if it is raining out. When leaving, the inner tent and gear can be packed away while sheltered under the still-erected outer tent. Secondly, you are not required to use the inner tent with such a design and have the freedom to use the outer shell only, potentially lightening your load even further and creating more space (so long as you don't mind any potential insects invading your space).

# Tent Entrance

The entrance of this tent faces off to the side. This tends to make it easier to lay out your gear appropriately and get in and out of the bedding easily. With tents having an entrance at the head end, you often have to crawl over your bedding to get in or out and will generally find yourself having a more awkward time storing and reaching your gear. Imagine yourself sitting with your feet out of the tent to remove muddy boots before having to reverse direction and crawl in feet-first. Tents with such an entrance are generally inefficient to use.

*The Complete Survival Shelters Handbook*

## Tent Accessories

**Elastic loops and guy-lines.** All tents will be fitted with elastic loops at the bottom edge of the cover. Most, if not all tents will also have guy-lines attached at strategic locations. In many scenarios, you will not have to use them unless you expect a stormy night.

**Vents and mosquito netting.** Tents are usually also equipped with one or more vents to allow moisture-laden air to escape and so keep condensation down. The inside cover of the tent will more than likely get soaked with condensation anyway, regardless of whether the vents are open or not. To prevent this, leave the tent door open whenever you can get away with it, and rely on the mosquito netting of the inner door instead to offer a sense of privacy/insulation.

## Drying Your Groundsheet and Outer Tent

In the morning, there will often be some moisture on the groundsheet and outer tent. If you have time, dry at least the inner tent/groundsheet before packing it away. You can attach the (wet) outer tent to the outside of your pack, either with available straps or with a pouch, preventing moisture inside of your pack.

## Fire Safety

A few words of caution when using tents in a wilderness situation. As the material of modern tents is usually extremely flammable, or at the very least, melts easily, it is important to keep the tent well away from fire. Also, as fresh air cannot be easily introduced, hot coals such as in a barbecue should never be brought into the tent. Every year, people die due to carbon monoxide poisoning after bringing disposable barbecues into the tent to provide warmth. The same applies to camping stoves and the like.

##  HAMMOCKS

Hammocks are truly unique shelters with a large number of benefits and very few drawbacks. Hammock camping is still relatively unknown but is becoming increasingly popular. Hammocks are now so much more than a net slung between two trees; they have become truly high-performing suspended tents.

When compared to a regular tent, hammocks present a number of important benefits. You don't need to search for flat, open ground to set up a hammock. All you need is two anchor points about 12 to 15 feet apart. These anchor points can be trees, fence poles, large boulders, vehicle roof racks or any combination of the above. With a hammock, it doesn't matter if the ground is wet or covered in snow. I've seen hammocks slung up above a swamp, with a canoe tethered underneath. Rocky or uneven ground or hillsides are not a problem when using a hammock. In fact, the ability to sling up a hammock in inhospitable terrain is a great asset if you wish to keep a lower profile. Being above ground, you're far away from annoying or potentially dangerous crawlers. By hanging your hammock higher up in the trees, you could even stay safe from other animals, such as wild dogs or (some) bears. Even if keeping a low profile or safety are not a concern, you will still have a far wider choice of campsites compared to a normal tent.

## Comfort

A hammock is not a compromise of comfort for lower equipment weight. The hammock is actually more comfortable than a normal tent. As you are above the ground, you do not have any problems with hard spots or uneven terrain features. This also means you won't need as thick a sleeping mat as the sleeping mat is now only there to insulate you from the cold rather than to provide padding over hard ground. When the hammock is of good design and correctly slung, and you adopt the right position, there is better and more flexible support for your body, which prevents stiffness and provides a generally more restful sleep since you won't roll around as much in search of comfort. The hammocks I use have a ridgeline running through them, ensuring that the internal space is always the same and allowing for the inevitable differences caused by setting the hammock up in different circumstances. In my experience, sleeping in a hammock allows me to wake truly refreshed each morning. I have never missed my bed at home when out with the hammock.

## Environmental Connection

The hammock allows a better connection with the environment around you while providing more than adequate shelter. In a tent, the level of awareness is generally quite low and any sounds heard during the night often remain unidentified. In some situations, if more investigation of the happenings around the tent is required, the unavoidable noise associated with getting out of the tent will draw unintended attention and highlight your position. In a hammock, you retain visibility of your surroundings because you can simply look around you when required without moving a muscle.

*The Complete Survival Shelters Handbook*

## Carrying and Storing

Hammocks are lightweight and pack up small as there are no poles to worry about. The Hennessy Hammocks photographed here weigh between 2 and 3 pounds. This includes the suspension, hammock (enclosed with mosquito netting) and flysheet. The hammock packs up in two long tubes called "snakeskins." These allow you to set up or take down the hammock within minutes. Some people like to use two sets of snakeskins; one for the hammock and one for the flysheet. Storing the flysheet in its own set of snakeskins allows you to tie it to the outside of your pack after a wet night.

One of the models visible in the photographs actually includes an extremely lightweight, reflective pad, which will remove the need for a separate sleeping pad.

Should you end up in an area where there are no suitable suspension points, you can actually set up the hammock on the ground with the aid of hiking poles or some shorter sticks, in which case the hammock will function in the same way a small hiking tent would, except for the heavy waterproof groundsheet. You may wish to put a tarp on the ground first if it's wet.

## Chair Functionality

While a tent is only for sleeping, the hammock can also be used as a chair while the flysheet will give you enough space to perform your daily chores out of the rain.

## Setting Up Your Hammock

Depending on the model, the hammock will need from 10 to 16 feet of space between the two anchor points. The hammocks I use from Hennessy Hammock come with tree straps. These straps provide convenient attachment points and help to avoid damaging the tree when tying the hammocks or leaving telltale signs of your presence after you've left. If your hammock doesn't come with straps like these, then you may be able to improvise some from webbing straps or old seatbelt straps.

A carabiner is useful to connect the hammock to the tree straps after wrapping them around the tree. Once you become used to the hammock, you will find your own preferred way of setting it up; the following instructions are best practice guidelines.

1. Suspend the hammock. Connect the head end of the hammock first to the tree strap, carabiner or tree itself with a temporary knot. Walk to the second tree and tie the foot end to the strap, carabiner or tree. Most people prefer to have the foot end slightly higher than the head end, in which case you'd want to ensure that the strap is 3 to 4 inches higher at the foot end compared to the head end. You want to make sure that the hammock hangs perfectly centered between the two trees, with a distinct drop in the middle. When there's weight in the hammock (put your pack in it) the angle of the two suspension ropes should be around 30 degrees off the horizontal dropping toward the center.

2. Retie your knots. When you're happy with the way the hammock is arranged, tie the knot at the head end off properly. While there are a number of suitable knots you can use, I recommend starting with the knots suggested by the manufacturer as they are designed with the type of suspension used in the hammock in mind.

3. Test the suspension. Carefully sit in the center of the hammock, gently committing your weight. The hammock will probably sag a little as the knots tighten and the materials stretch. Get back out again and have a look at how the hammock now hangs. Double-check to make sure the knots are still good.

4. Install the flysheet. Attach the flysheet to the little hooks provided on the suspension cord, and slide the hooks out so the flysheet is tightened between foot and head end and centered over the hammock.

5. Tie off the flysheet. Now, unroll your flysheet and attach the cords provided to tie-off points on other trees or to pegs in the ground. When there's fairly little wind, I prefer to tie the

flysheet off to trees or guide it over sticks in the ground so the pitch of the flysheet on both sides of the hammock is fairly minimal. This allows me the most freedom of movement, gives the most space underneath and enables me to look around when lying in the hammock. When it's stormy out or if there's heavy rain, I will tie the flysheet directly to pegs in the ground. This will provide much more protection as the pitch of the flysheet will be much steeper, though it will cost me in available space.

6. Finish the hammock set-up. Finally, attach the hammock tie-outs to the flysheet to spread out the hammock. As a handy addition for rainy weather, Hennessy Hammock provides two small funnels that clip onto the O-rings and screw onto most basic soda bottles. The rain will run down the flysheet and be guided into the bottles. This is handy as a water source but also because the added weight will help keep the fly tensioned as it will stretch a bit when getting wet.

## How to Lie in a Hammock

For ultimate comfort, you have to lie diagonally across a hammock. The models shown in these images, for instance, accommodate this position by providing a tie-off toward the foot end on the right side (viewed when lying on your back) and toward the head end on the left side, creating an asymmetrical space. When lying in the hammock, place your feet toward the right side of the hammock and your shoulders to the left. You will notice immediately that the hammock will shape around you in such a way to allow you to lie nearly flat. As long as you lie along that diagonal, it doesn't matter if you sleep on your back or curled up on your side.

When lying in a sleeping bag, the part of the bag underneath you will compress and will not insulate very well at all. During very warm nights, this isn't a problem, but when the temperature starts to drop, you may want to insert a traditional sleeping mat over this diagonal. This may be a little awkward at first, but after a few nights, you'll soon get the hang of placing everything just right for going to sleep.

In the photographs below, one hammock has a bottom opening while the other has a strong zipper running along one side. With the zipped one, you can easily lay your mat and sleeping bag in the right position, undress, and slip in. With a bottom-entry hammock, you will also be able to do this once you're used to it; however, at first, it's handiest to position the sleeping mat correctly, undress, and then step into the sleeping bag before getting into the hammock.

The first hammock pictured here is actually double-layered, with space to slip in a sleeping mat or a reflective bubble pad. The benefit is that the pad doesn't move around during the night, which can sometimes cause the pad to pop out from under you. Because the pad is suspended below you, you also have more freedom to move around without having to make sure you're still lying on the pad. The reflective bubble pad provided by Hennessy Hammock as an alternative to a sleeping mat is actually an ingenious idea. The bubbles provide still air for insulation and the silver coating bounces any radiant heat back to you. It is cheap and incredibly lightweight. I found that it packs up smaller than a regular sleeping mat too. In the past, I have also used regular floor carpet cut to size instead of sleeping mats, which was extremely warm and comfortable but a bit on the heavy side.

The other hammock pictured has a second cloth layer suspended below the hammock, with a layer of foam topped by an emergency blanket inserted between the two. This method works extremely well but is a little noisy until you've settled down properly. Again, it avoids the need to carry a separate sleeping mat.

I have seen other people use old sleeping bags or blankets suspended below the hammock in order to avoid having to bring a sleeping mat. There are many different options. The best thing to do is to simply test out what works best for you.

Inside the hammock, you will find a ridgeline, which is handy for hanging items onto. I usually leave my pack below the hammock and fold up my clothes to form a pillow.

# NET HAMMOCKS

If you decide to try out or purchase a hammock, do not look for the classic, quintessential net hammock suspended between two spreader bars as they are uncomfortable and can tip over. These net hammocks were designed with the appearance of a flat surface to lie on to make traditional hammocks appealing to Westerners during the last century. Although the design is seriously flawed, they caught on in photographs and holiday marketing to such an extent that the very image of the net hammock between two palm trees automatically springs to mind when hearing the word "relaxation" or "beach holiday." With a bit of looking around, you will find hammocks such as the Hennessy ones I use which are modeled after the original aboriginal hammocks but redesigned especially for camping. They are extremely comfortable, durable shelters which also eliminate the danger of tipping over or falling out.

In the past, I used to provide all my course participants with a hammock. I often came across people who were nervous with the idea of hanging suspended between two trees. However, after a couple of nights in the hammock, they would often want one for themselves. It does take a night or two to get the hang of. Your first night may be a bit less comfortable, but with experience, you'll be able to set up the hammock in just the right way to provide you with a more comfortable night's sleep than you've ever had in the outdoors.

*The* Complete Survival Shelters *Handbook*

## BIVVY BAG

A bivvy bag is simply a small, light but durable waterproof bag, which acts as an alternative to a tent. Bivvy bags are commonly used to avoid the weight or size of a hiking tent in their pack, or as an emergency alternative in a bug out bag. Unlike hiking tents or hammocks, the bivvy bag only allows space for sleeping as it is just slightly bigger than a sleeping bag. The bivvy bag is more useful when constantly on the move. The bivvy bag is typically a lot lighter to carry than a tent or hammock and takes up little space as it is smaller and doesn't always require zippers, mesh and other materials a tent or hammock requires. It is a lot smaller when in use, allowing you to take advantage of smaller sites and retain a low profile where required.

There are different types of bivvy bags available from basic lightweight and mosquito-net-only bags to the heavier, more advanced models designed for more extended use and heavier weather, with poles to keep the bag off your face. Which type suits you best depends on your circumstances and intended use.

When you're planning the purchase of a bivvy bag, there are a few criteria you need to keep in mind.

- It is important you get as useful a bag with as minimal a weight and pack size as possible, yet retain the protection you require. For instance, if you plan to use a bag during heavier weather and for extended periods of time, you may wish to use one where a pole holds the fabric off your face. Alternatively, you may appreciate a lighter bag with mesh sewn into the material at face level to help vent moisture if you are in a dry climate.
- The bag needs to be weatherproof. What this means to you depends a bit on your environment.
- The bag needs to give you as much comfort as possible. You'll want a bag that remains dry inside and evaporates sweat easily. Perhaps in some climates, you only require a bag to keep the bugs off, in which case you can purchase a mosquito net bivvy. You need to consider how much space there is inside. Can you move around a little? Is there space for your gear? (If not, bring a separate bag for your backpack.) Can you bring a sleeping mat inside?
- You want the material to be durable. If you need to camp in an area with sharp stones, thorns or similar terrain, a super-lightweight bag may get damaged and let water in. Many bags provide a breathable, lightweight upper portion and use heavier materials for the bottom. Many bivvy bags contain zippers. As these will be used a lot, you'll want to make sure they're sturdy and don't catch the fabric.

Typically, if your bag is made out of breathable material such as Gore-Tex fabric, it will help reduce condensation, but still not eliminate it altogether. Managing the entrance helps to vent the rest of the moisture. Ideally, when using a bivvy bag, you'll want to keep the entrance as open as possible. For this reason, a lot of bivvy-campers will set up a small tarp over their head end so the bivvy bag only covers from the shoulders down while the tarp covers from mid-waist to above the head. This method often also allows some extra space for your equipment.

Even though the bag is waterproof, you still want to avoid lying in puddles, seeking instead as much natural shelter as possible while avoiding any hazards as discussed before. As you are only covered by the most minimal of shelters, a good site is extra important.

# ✦— BELL TENT —✦

Bell tents are often incorrectly marketed as lavvus. This is in part to give them more of an ethnic appeal, but also because the shape so closely resembles the lavvu's. The main difference is that the bell tent only has one supporting pole in the center, rather than the 11 or more poles used in the lavvu. For this reason, the bell tent also does not have a smoke hole, though it does have a rather sizeable vent, which can be opened or closed as desired through the use of strings.

I have seen people using small, open fires in a bell tent, but with the size of the vent, I would be extremely cautious and perhaps opt for a small, wood-burning stove instead. If this is what you intend to do, ensure the tent you purchase is adapted for the use of a wood burner, with fireproof material separating the canvas from the stove flue.

Modern Store-Bought Shelters

# Setting Up the Tent

1. Setting up the bell tent is fairly easy. Lay the canvas out in the circle formed by its bottom edge and peg it to the ground in such a way that the circle is taut all the way around. Be sure to orient the doorway in the desired direction before you do so.

2. Once you're happy with the footprint and all the pegs are secure, unzip the entrance and crawl inside with the assembled pole. Place the tip of the pole in the space provided at the tip of the tent, and push the pole up until it can stand upright, exactly vertical below the tip of the tent.

3. When you don't have a wood burner, you can lay out your internal space any way you wish. If you do have one, you'll find it's usually nicest to place your bedding so the stove is between you and the doorway.

Quality bell tents are usually a bit pricier, but this is because the design requires strong cloth and excellent seams to retain its shape and durability. In return, you get a large tent with ample space inside to live in comfort. It may well be worth it to bring a tarp to sit and lie on, though, as these tents usually do not include groundsheets. There's also no protection from mosquitoes or other bugs as there is no bug-proof inner tent. Due to its solid construction and ability to accept a wood burner inside, this tent can be quite usable in extremely cold or snowy conditions. Depending on the design of the tent, you may be able to travel without the pole, and fashion your own when out in the wilderness. However, there is little flexibility with the length, so you may wish to attach a non-stretching string to the tent to represent the exact length of the manufactured pole.

*The Complete Survival Shelters Handbook*

# Chapter 5

# Mental Preparedness

As anyone can see when glancing through this book, its pages are filled to the brim with physical skills that can be learned to aid the outdoorsman or wilderness skills enthusiast. Obviously, many of these skills are extremely important to survival. However, being able to perform them well and reliably in energy-sapping cold weather or searing hot, willpower-draining desert conditions is but one of the pillars of survival. This chapter attempts to deal with the other pillar—your mental and emotional attitude.

Your brain is, after all, your biggest resource for information. For survival knowledge, intuition, judgment or capability for forward thinking, it's clear that the brain is the key to survival. Unfortunately, just like a strained wrist will negatively impact a canoeist's performance, a brain affected by stress or panic will negatively impact your chances of staying alive in difficult situations or your comfort level and enjoyment in less extreme situations. Learned information stored in the brain can become difficult to access during extremely urgent situations, leaving the individual to rely more on instincts. The trick is to interrupt this natural tendency for the brain to revert back to instinct and access the survival knowledge learned instead.

Learning the physical skills contained in this book to a fair degree of mastery is not extremely difficult for a dedicated practitioner. Unfortunately, though, it is much harder to train in mental skills.

Armed forces worldwide experience the difficulty of training recruits for real-life combat. The main method they use, drilling, will also partially equip you with the mental skills needed to survive. I say partly because more is needed.

You also need a real understanding of the emotions and stresses involved as well as thorough knowledge of how you respond in certain situations; in other words, you must know your weaknesses and strengths. Immersing yourself in practice scenarios in as big a range of climates as possible under controlled conditions is the key.

Such exercises will also provide you with another important gift in the form of confidence while weeding out arrogance or overconfidence.

Finally, mastering a few simple tricks when entering a real-life situation will allow you to adopt the needed mental attitude for survival.

Let's cover these four subjects of mental survival skills in more detail.

# Drilling

Drilling might seem straightforward, but it is not. It requires you to generate the motivation and discipline not simply to learn a skill set, but to get on the path to absolute mastery. In my opinion, you can consider yourself to have learned a skill if you can perform it with a 95 percent success rate under controlled conditions. Real mastery of a skill means you can perform it with a variety of materials (even if you don't always know the material) during a range of circumstances so wide that you can almost say you could perform that skill any time, anywhere.

Let's take the debris hut covered on page 25 for instance:

Learning the skill means that with a large number of resources, you're able to build the shelter within 4 to 5 hours when the weather is warm and dry and you're able to do this 9 to 10 times out of 10 attempts. When you sleep in it, you will be relatively comfortable.

Mastering the skill means you're also able to build that shelter 9 to 10 out of 10 attempts and survive the night in relative comfort; however, you can do this in adverse weather conditions in an environment where you don't really have enough resources and have to think out of the box in order to construct a workable shelter.

Not every skill you have knowledge of needs to be mastered. It is sufficient for most of your skill set to simply be learned. In fact, after years of learning and teaching these skills, I can emphatically say that a great number of the skills I know are merely on the road to true mastery, each skill on different steps of the ladder, while some skills are only barely learned. For instance, I'm hardly an expert on felting wool, though I have learned to perform the task. I've pushed only a few of my skills to near mastery—these constitute the skills I feel are most vital in a survival situation and include such abilities as shelter-building and fire-lighting. As time goes on, other, lower priority skills (closely tied to my level of interest) are slowly advanced toward mastery. I strongly believe that what makes a great wilderness practitioner is the ability to become a jack-of-all-trades, yet still be a master of some. The "some" is decided through the close examination of your own priorities.

Learning a skill and mastering a skill are not completely different entities. They are both markers on the same sliding scale. First, a debris hut is learned under comfortable conditions, then, it is slept in and improved. Perhaps the next time, you will build one during the colder season, sleeping in it, improving it. During another opportunity, you might decide to arrive closer to dusk, or use an area with less resources available. The point is to constantly raise the challenge level. I cannot tell you how many times you should build that shelter to achieve mastery. Keep raising the level of adversity. The true test of whether you achieved another level of mastery is whether the shelter was good enough to allow you to sleep comfortably through the night. If it wasn't, figure out how to improve the situation and test it again until you get it right before moving on to a more difficult challenge.

# Understanding Emotions and Stresses

This area covers both the mental ups and downs. While the other three subjects covered here will help combat the extremes, a good understanding of how the brain works in these situations can be immensely helpful.

Finding yourself in an unexpected survival situation can be an extremely stressful and frightening experience that can easily lead to panic and hysteria. Even simply getting lost can cause anxiety. Compound that with the realization that survival is at stake as well as possible adverse conditions, such as injuries or weather, and the chances of getting into a panic increase substantially.

When faced with a life-threatening situation, the brain triggers the release of hormones, such as adrenaline and cortisol, to set the body up for the fight-or-flight response. Kept under control, these hormones will be useful. Adrenaline-boosted heart function triggers the release of stored energy and sends increased amounts of blood to the larger muscle groups while bringing the environment into clearer focus and giving the sense that time slows down. Cortisol limits the energy normally spent on non-vital organs such as digestion. (Hence the feeling of an unsettled stomach after an "adrenaline rush.") These effects can help you get to immediate safety or build that crucial shelter as it causes you to perform at peak performance.

The trade-off is that when in this state, you expend huge amounts of energy, which will have to be replenished through sleep, water and food. In some instances, allowing yourself to remain in this state for any length of time can actually decrease your longer-term survival odds due to an inability to replenish the energy consumed. Fine motor skills and situational awareness suffer as well in this state, which can cause accidents. Basically, while in this state, your body and brain think big rather than small.

When left out of control, this state of mind can lead to panic and the expenditure of energy on useless activities such as running away from a situation that doesn't require running away from, performing useless tasks or hysteria. In the longer term, cortisol can deteriorate your mental attitude and increase a feeling of hopelessness.

Feeling down can be caused by a variety of factors. This includes spending too much energy on your fight-or-flight response while not being able to replenish it fast enough. Trying to stay in control of the fight-or-flight response should help with that.

Another factor could be the lack of enough food, water or rest.

Yet another factor is an emotional difficulty to accept the reality of the circumstances. This is actually incredibly common; I have observed it in myself and others even during some of my courses. It is the one factor that can be covered by immersing yourself in practice situations.

As part of my curriculum, I take people out for a week-long experience in the woods without any tools or equipment except the clothes on our backs. During these sessions, the areas where the brain struggles to accept the situation become obvious to participants. It starts with really silly things, such as a reluctance or even inability to defecate or urinate until one can physically no longer stop it. It seems to me that some people find it difficult to break through that barrier of pooing while not having a clean toilet with toilet paper and four privacy-protecting walls. I should admit that at times I have also "deferred the act" to a later time, thinking of the "inconveniences," knowing full well that there was no practical reason for doing so. More serious are instances where people simply can't stomach eating that wild squirrel (I sympathize as would many of my past course participants) or those unfamiliar-tasting but edible plants. In these cases, people usually manage to eat some wild foods, but either not enough, or too late, impacting too much on available energy reserves and causing me to have to "cheat" by importing some modern foods into the experience in order to prevent a waste of the learning experience or worse, physical or mental harm.

Again, immersing yourself in exactly those experiences can teach you not only where your demons lie, but the discipline to overcome them. Having to exit such an experience should not be seen as a failure, but a lesson. The next time, you will be better able to produce the discipline required to push through those barriers. In that sense, it's much like physical conditioning.

# Gaining Confidence

This is the easier mental skill to train for as it will be produced automatically as part of the process of learning wilderness skills. However, arrogance or its milder cousin, overconfidence, can be the cause of not only physical danger, but longer-term mental health as well. If you thought that you had mastered building that shelter when in reality, you only learned the skill, the inability of building that shelter in a wilderness situation can leave you exposed to hypothermia as well as frustration or depression. To some extent, this can happen to anyone, including the most seasoned wilderness instructor. This is one of the many reasons why complex tasks are usually completed only once the most basic and needed ones are carried out. Not one wilderness instructor I know will tell you not to build a good shelter first.

As I already stated earlier, drilling and immersion experience will greatly help prevent such a scenario. Studying your circumstances and prioritizing properly will help take care of the rest.

# Adopting the Right Mental Attitude

When faced with a survival situation, take the following simple steps to help set yourself up mentally for the journey ahead.

**Recognize that panic is possible**—Spend a moment recognizing your level of panic. Assess it, use it. Accept that a sense of panic is part of the process, but that you cannot allow it to consume you. When you are able to recognize and accept your feelings, you will allow them to be a part of you rather than giving the panic energy by fighting it.

**Face your problems one by one**—Don't look at all your problems as one, big, giant problem. Rather than facing the whole survival situation, take a step back, set some immediate priorities, and then view them as small, independent problems. Many of these problems can wait. Solving all these individual problems one by one is the solution to the puzzle of survival. In fact, rather than calling them problems, you could refer to them as roadblocks, challenges or barriers. These words suggest obstacles that can be broken through, navigated around or simply ignored altogether, whereas "problems" is a more negative word implying that solutions may not always exist and that you can't move forward unless such a problem is solved. A 100-mile walk is never conquered in one giant leap. It's conquered one step at a time.

**Lay out and keep an inventory of any equipment or random items you have**—This serves both as a useful (mental) list of resources, but also forces your brain to slow down.

Keep a positive and upbeat approach. Make jokes with yourself (or others when present), and reflect on how much water you currently have in the glass. If you got to this stage, you're obviously alive. Start from there and add any successes to the tally.

**Focus on your tasks**—Do not allow your mind to wander too much. It's not healthy initially to spend all your time thinking of that hamburger or shower or how much you miss people close to you. There will be plenty of time for such reflections later. On the other hand, visualizing the desired outcome and dreaming of successfully navigating the journey can be helpful

Surprisingly enough, these techniques are often needed during self-imposed survival experiences as much as they would be during actual emergencies.

I cannot stress enough that simply reading this book is not sufficient (that would equate to overconfidence). The mental aspects of wilderness living are as much a skill as building an excellent shelter. It has to be mastered. You have to drill and immerse yourself. Finding your own boundaries and experiencing the things you struggle with are extremely important. A total level of honesty with yourself is required. You can seriously impair your survival or even enjoyment of these skills if you are lying to yourself about your level of competence.

Finally, keep in mind that many of the shelters described in this book use a lot of natural resources and may damage an environment. When practicing or trying out these designs, do it in such a way to minimize the impact on the area. Afterward, always level the site so it looks the same way it did when you arrived. Also keep in mind that there may be laws or regulations you have to adhere to. So, when planning a trip to practice the skills described in this book, always read up on any laws and rules that apply to the area you're going into. In some countries, there's a "ramblers right of way" over private land. This benefit can only be maintained when people crossing into these properties leave no trace of their presence and ask permission to camp wherever possible.

# Index

## F

Fight-or-flight response, 137
Fire safety, 13–14, 46, 122, 133
Fireplaces, in debris shelters, 60–61
Firewood, 61–62
Fleece clothing, 6, 7; safety, 6
Floor plans. *See specific shelter types*
Foam mats, 10
Focus, and survival situations, 139
Foil blankets, 10; as shelter, 73–74
Footwear, 8–9

## G

Gers (yurts), as shelter, 91–116; constructing, 91–115; usage, 115–16
Gloves, 9
Grass mattresses, in debris shelters, 64–65
Grommets, homemade, 78
Ground sheet, drying, 121

## H

Hammer making, 19
Hammocks: net, 129; as shelter, 123–30
Hand tools, 18
Hats, 9
Heat loss, 4
Hiking tents, as shelter, 118–22; accessories, 121

## I

Insulation: and clothing, 6, 8; in debris huts, 29–30, 31–32; in gers, 116; in snow shelters, 58–59

## J

Jeans, 6

## K

Khanas (yurt walls), 93–96

## L

Lamps, tallow, 67–68
Lavvus, as shelter, 79–90; constructing, 80–88; materials, 80; setting up, 88–90; usage, 90
Layering clothing, and heat management, 5–7
Lean-tos, hand-built, 34–36
Leaves, as shelter material, 14–15. *See also* Debris huts
Lighting: tallow lamps, 67–68
Linen clothing, 6
Location, of shelters, 12–14. *See also specific shelter types*
Logs, as shelter material, 14

## M

Mats, sleeping, 10
Mattresses, grass, in debris shelters, 64–65
Mental preparedness, 135–40
Mid-layer clothing, 6–7
Modern material shelters, 70–116
Mongolian yurts, as shelter, 91–116; constructing, 91–115; materials, 92–93; usage, 115–16
Mummy bags, 11